HOW (NOT) TO
BUILD A
GREAT TEAM

FROM THE **HOW-NOT-TO GUIDES FOR LEADERS** SERIES

HOW (NOT) TO BUILD A GREAT TEAM

MARY E. MARSHALL & KIM OBBINK

Indigo River Publishing

How (NOT) To Build A Great Team

© 2020 by Mary E. Marshall and Kim Obbink

Edited by Tanner Chau, Joshua Owens, and Regina Cornell
Cover and interior design by Robin Vuchnich
Illustrations by Robin Vuchnich

Indigo River Publishing
3 West Garden Street, Ste. 718
Pensacola, FL 32502
www.indigoriverpublishing.com

Ordering Information:

Quantity sales: Special discounts are available on quantity purchases by corporations, associations, and others. For details, contact the publisher at the address above.

Orders by US trade bookstores and wholesalers: Please contact the publisher at the address above.

Printed in the United States of America

Library of Congress Control Number: 2019957538

ISBN: 978-1-950906-41-3 (paperback), 978-1-950906-40-6 (ebook)

First Edition

With Indigo River Publishing, you can always expect great books, strong voices, and meaningful messages. Most importantly, you'll always find...words worth reading.

CONTENTS

SECTION 3

ABOUT THE AUTHORS

PREFACE

***How (NOT) To Build A Great Team* is the second in a series of how-not-to guides for leaders and managers,** and like our first book, *How (NOT) To Be A Leader*, it is a quick-read collection of hilarious cautionary tales that we hope will help you avoid some of the more obvious speed bumps and traps along your leadership journey.

We believe that every business is a people business. It is the employees, the talented and skilled individuals and teams, that are the central nervous system of every business's operation and strategy. Having great people allows leaders to keep their sights set on the day-to-day business itself and on the broader space of an industry. By doing so, they can focus on product, competitive strategies, sales, and innovation. If you are constantly churning around in the mucky mess of people and HR issues, the world outside the walls of your business will rush by you—and you'll still be trying to figure out a way to fire Samantha without hurting her feelings.

Dealing with people is not for the faint of heart. It is where the toughest conversations occur, the most complex interpersonal dynamics exist, and where you'll be called upon to be psychiatrist, HR professional, mediator, referee, umpire, teacher, and camp counselor. It is where you can do the most damage by making bad decisions, where the wrong people can have the most lasting negative impact, and where bad people quickly kill healthy company cultures.

It can also be the most rewarding. When you experience the positive impact that well-developed and well-managed people and teams have on your business, and when you witness the personal and professional growth of the people you've hired, you've arrived at people management nirvana. You and your business will be rewarded with a happy culture, good employee-retention, and a reputation that will attract top talent from across your industry. Plus, it will just feel good.

In this book, we will address three critical aspects of developing a great team: hiring and firing, team management, and leadership development. We'll share with you some real and some entirely made-up stories about hiring the wrong people for the wrong reasons, how easy it is to create a dysfunctional team of do-nothings, and what to do when what was once your brilliant entrepreneurial vision suddenly turns into the lost chapter of *Lord of the Flies*.

Buckle up, leader. This is where the going gets tough.

SECTION 1

HIRE SLOW, FIRE FAST

Interviewing candidates—you either love it or you hate it. Well guess what, if you hate it, you'd better start loving it because it's one of the most important things you can do to build a great team. And to build great teams within your organization, it is not something you can outsource. Great leaders are constantly recruiting. Whether you have a job opening or not, you should always be on the lookout for top talent. We'd go as far as to say that networking for talent is even more important than networking for new business.

But successful hiring isn't a signed offer letter—it's a process. How often have you heard, "We're gonna throw 'em in the deep end and see if they float," or "We're desperate; we just need someone that can fog a mirror"? Ugh. Successful hiring means going through a thoughtful and thorough process on the front end, and that process takes time. Bad hiring decisions come from informal processes, snap decisions, decisions made in a void, and decisions based on emotions or gut feelings rather than a true understanding of what's needed from a candidate whose talents and skills are aligned with the job or team.

But even with the most thoughtful and rigorous hiring practices, we all make mistakes. We hire the wrong people for the job, and they take jobs that are wrong for them. It's a two-way street. But unlike the thoughtful, time-intensive hiring process, when you've got the wrong person in the wrong job, and you feel your organization has done a fair job of trying to address performance issues, time is of the essence.

Are you hiring too fast because you think you've found a unicorn of an employee and are worried that he'll take another job? Hiring your brother's whiny daughter for an internship instead of a qualified junior sales person (that you can train to be a leader) because you are a nice guy or can't say no? And conversely, are you firing too slow because you can't take the tears or simply don't have a proper performance-management process in place? If so, this section is for you.

Hiring and firing is the best and the worst part of leadership. No one likes firing people. Good leaders never like firing people. But good leaders do understand the risks of avoiding it when it's necessary.

CHAPTER 1

AVAILABILITY IS NOT A SKILL

THE AVAILABILITY METHOD

From the desk of the snarky, inexperienced recruiter: As a leader, it's always tough to find great talent. Because of this, one of the most important things to consider is whether or not the person is actually available when you need them. What this means is that you need to pay attention to the ones that are available precisely when you need them. It's better to have this as a criterion than to actually go out and find someone who won't come to work for you anyway. I call this successful method of hiring the Availability Method.

I discovered the Availability Method the hard way while dealing with an HR manager who was always trying to use recruiters (who, by the way, are very expensive), and then she would delay hiring anyone because she said the talent pool was not very good. I kept telling her that I wanted to hire someone NOW. Getting my position filled was much more important to me than waiting for the exact right person, knowing that might never happen. I can make people into what they should be, so I'm not waiting around for the perfect prince or princess. Who needs the best when good enough will do?

I instructed her that she had two weeks to find candidates for me and I was going to hire from that bunch—and they all better be available! I also let her know that I was done paying ridiculous recruiting fees when all they did was place ads and not much else. I gave her the impression that her job might be the next to be replaced if she didn't stop dragging her feet looking for that perfect candidate. Let's get on with it! One of my great skills as a leader is my decisiveness and ability to make decisions quickly. People frequently admire me for it.

So, after two weeks she presented me with three candidates, and none of them were what anyone would call stellar, but they were all available! I sorted through them, interviewed them, and—all things being equal—I hired the one who said she didn't need to give two weeks' notice to her current employer. That's my kind of availability!

I needed someone who could start right away and hit the ground running. She started the following Monday, and as far as I know, she's doing OK. It takes time to learn some of our systems and processes, so I'm sure she'll learn what she needs to in time. That's what I call fast hiring based on availability. If they have the right skills and aren't available, what does it matter?

This seems so obvious, but I have to repeat myself multiple times. The other way this can be a great leadership lesson is to grab up any good person who comes your way *when they're available*, even if you don't have a spot.

No time like the present to grab up top talent. I hired someone on the spot this way about six months ago, and he has fit right into the team. I did find out later that he was fired from his last position and the reason is a little sketchy, *but* I find that it's best not to ask too many questions. You might actually have to deal with it if you find something that you're not happy with. That's business. In this case, it's really true that ignorance is bliss!

Don't worry if you hire someone not quite right for the role when using the Availability Method, because you'll have someone to take their place in no time if you adhere to the method. It's not a failure; it's fast hiring and it works! Turnover is good. Knowing I don't mind firing them keeps people from getting stale, and on their toes. Some will tell you that there is so much more to hiring, but I've found I can train for almost everything, and if not...let 'em go. There are plenty more fish in the sea if you believe there are and adhere to the Availability Method of hiring!

LET'S GET REAL

Hiring someone based on the fact that they are available is like hiring the house painter to cut your hair because he has a few hours between jobs. It's not likely to turn out well for either of you. We've seen this used as the deciding factor in so many hiring decisions, and it shouldn't be, or at the very least it should be at the bottom of the list.

If you hire with only availability in mind, you will potentially be hiring the best of the worst, which means they ultimately won't work out. You'll eventually downgrade your entire team. Oftentimes the reason they're available is that they got fired, quit, or are otherwise not a great candidate for any job, let alone the one you're hiring for.

First, create a great job description with required and desired skills, characteristics, and experience. Then create interview questions around values. Interview for cultural fit, test for skills and a willingness to learn what they may need to, and then ascertain if they're available. If you pick the weaker candidate because they're available before the better one, you will regret it down the road. **There is almost no position for which not filling it immediately will be catastrophic for the organization.**

Availability is good only if all the other hiring factors are in place—a match for skills, job description, culture, values, experience, and compensation scale. Then, and only then, if all is equal, would you want to consider availability as a factor. Last, not first. In some cases, you can entice the right candidate to leave their current job, but only if the package you are offering is consistent with your compensation practices. Creating a great team starts with your ability to attract and retain good talent; it doesn't have anything to do with how quickly you do it based on the availability of C players.

CHAPTER 2

IT'S OK, JUST THIS ONCE

NOTES FOR UPCOMING BOOK ON LEADERSHIP:

From the desk of the tone-deaf leader: When hiring, way too much value is placed on values. (Ohh, that's a great title! Man, I'm so clever!) This seems to be the new buzzword, but frankly, it's completely overrated. My experience has been that people tell you things about their values but don't really mean them. I mean, let's get real, who among us hasn't eaten the fruit and veggies at the grocery store, or not returned money when they undercharge you? It's the grocery store, after all, and they make plenty of money. And I hate that ridiculous saying that your real values show up when no one is looking—if no one is looking, it absolutely doesn't count. I counter that if a tree falls in the woods and no one hears it, did it really happen? My point made.

However, because it's the latest craze in hiring and "culture," we have to at least pretend we're paying attention to it.

So figure out your value words, plaster them all over the place, and then hire based on some of these values but certainly don't make it the top priority. It's one of the surface things that you need to "show," but doing anything about it is a completely different animal. Just slow your roll on that one.

To prove my point, we just hired this great guy for sales. He was the top producer at his last company, one of our competitors, and we scooped him up as soon as he was available. Not really sure why he had to leave that company, and quite frankly, don't care because he's so good. After I hired him, he told me he knew the other candidate that we had been considering, and he'd made an anonymous call to the guy's wife to tell her bad things about our company. After my initial shock, he explained that he'd wanted the other candidate to drop out so he could get the job—I loved it! No wonder he was a winner. I love the creativity.

And creativity is one of our values, so score one for me on hiring this guy. Now, we also have a value of collaboration, which means he needs to work well with others, and that's not going as well as I had hoped. However, he's bringing in the numbers, so I don't care much about everyone liking him. It's not as important as getting those sales. Numbers trump everything in this business. I just need to work with him a little and teach him how to collaborate in a way that looks like he's being a team player. Then no one will care what he's doing behind the scenes to make the deals happen. Trying to collaborate is as good as I need to see.

UPDATE TO NOTES:

Unfortunately, I had to let my star sales guy go today. It was such a hard thing to do, but when the police showed up and shared with us that he had been selling some of our systems outside of the company, I really didn't have a choice. I had initiated the investigation but certainly didn't expect it to come back to Jack. He was such a superstar! He was doing so well, bringing the numbers in, and he was absolutely collaborating with the team; they even mentioned it to me. Of course, a couple of the other managers were questioning some of the sales tactics he was using and whether or not we really had signed sales orders for some of these products. Well, you can't win 'em all!

I still won't change my hiring practices, because deep down I know this guy was a winner. His only problem was the dumbass got caught. With just a little more time, I could have shown him how to win without getting into trouble. That requires just a little ingenuity and creativity, like he showed by knocking off that other sales candidate. Hmm, I wonder if that guy is still available.

Of course, I guess I should be honest, and we did lose another really good sales person and one inside person who tried to tell me what this guy was doing. But this is what happens when you hire superstars: the rest of the team gets jealous and tries to get you to fire them. Results over values every day!

LET'S GET REAL

Surprisingly, the above really did happen. And it happens more than you might imagine. Values are on display every day in a person's behavior, and if we ignore it, it's at our own peril. When it comes to hiring, it can be catastrophic for the organization to ignore.

The belief is that "just this once" we'll make the exception to hire a person who really doesn't exhibit a key value of the organization. However, it is never just this once. How many times do you take only one chip from a potato chip bag? You always go for a second. Behavior follows beliefs and beliefs follow values. You can change a behavior and train a skill as long as they are not tied to a deeply rooted value. It's like trying to change a very religious person away from their faith—it won't happen. So why do we often think we can do this in the workplace?

Because in the hiring phase we're still on the honeymoon and it's usually fun and games. We're still filled with hope, the adrenaline is pumping, and there could be a full-on hurricane going on outside and we wouldn't notice, let alone care. But we have to look to the marriage phase of having an employee; you won't have fun every day—or even every week or month or year. Anyone can do something for a short period of time that might be against who they really are. Asking them to do it over a long stretch of time will ultimately reveal who that person is and what their values are.

"Just this once"—ignoring values in the hiring—will lead to another, and another, and before long you will have eaten a whole bag of chips and feel bloated and bad. The consequence to the organization is a bunch of cultural misfits that will simply operate as who they are, not who you want them to be.

CHAPTER 3

TOO CLOSE TO HOME: HIRING IS RELATIVE

Sent: August 25, 3:00 p.m.
From: Karen, Founder
To: John, CEO
Subject: My Brother-in-Law

John,

I realize we don't have any open positions in the warehouse right now and that I've been asked pretty specifically not to get involved in hiring or staff decisions, but I've got a huge favor to ask. My brother-in-law, Kenny, is a terrific guy and is looking for a job. He's been down on his luck for the past ten or fifteen years as he got mixed up in some shady business a while back at his previous job. He and my sister are divorced now, but I always liked Kenny, and I feel like we could really help with his re-entry into society if we offer him a job. I'll take full responsibility for it, and the team doesn't need to know anything about his personal life or the assault/burglary conviction. He deserves a second chance. Let's do it.

He can start on Monday and report to Mike. I'm sure Mike will understand and you'll do a great job of explaining it to him.

Karen

Oh, most definitely, this is a terrific idea! You own the company and can do whatever you want. So, go for it. Jobs are hard to come by, and you've got plenty of them to go around, so be sure to put your friends and family at the top of the list—especially the ones that would have a hard time finding a job anywhere else. Providing jobs for your inner circle will make you feel good about yourself, secure your position as family matriarch or patriarch, and allow you to assert control over your friends and family. An important part of being a good leader is *totally* blurring the lines between business and personal. For you, it's ALL business, all of the time! If you can use your friends and family to help boost your bottom line, by all means do so.

Just like there is always a job for the hanger-on-er, there is always a job that can be created for any member of your family. The rest of your staff will be impressed by your loyalty to your family and your gigantic generous heart, particularly if your family member has no skills, relevant experience, or subject-matter expertise to contribute. If you experience any backlash from your employees, be sure to use your company values as an excuse for your decisions. For instance, if "learning" is one of your company values, you can simply explain that you've hired an individual with no experience to help employees learn more about things that have nothing to do with your business. "Expanding our horizons," as they say.

If you're hiring family members that may seem riskier than others, like Kenny, explain it away by saying you'll take responsibility for anything that goes wrong, but do everything in your power to keep any family skeletons squarely in the closet! One of the many benefits of hiring friends and family that would have a hard time finding work elsewhere is that you can pay them well below the pay grade for that position. Quid pro quo.

Your hiring managers can't say no; it's your company and you can do what you want. After all, hiring unqualified family and friends makes you a huge hero in your eyes. And that's a win-win for you!

LET'S GET REAL

This is a tricky one, so let's unpack it.

While there are many family-run businesses that have been well run and successful for generations, there are probably just as many that have failed as a business or caused huge fissures in the family. Those examples aside, there are private and public businesses that are not family run and have no preconceived requirements to hire or employ members of a biological family. It's our belief that in these businesses, **hiring family and friends should be avoided at all costs.** Like plague-level avoidance. It simply never works out in the long run.

More often than not, the fact that a family member or friend is available for a position seems to take precedence over their qualifications. Unless you had already instituted a work-release program in your organization, you wouldn't hire Kenny if he was a complete stranger, so why hire Kenny since he's family? It may be good for Kenny, but it's not good for your company. Your duty is to the company. Regarding Kenny's situation specifically: Please remember there are organizations and services qualified and trained to assist employees with special circumstances and needs. The ability to write a paycheck does not qualify you as an employment specialist for people with these or other types of extenuating circumstances.

On the other hand, if the family member or friend is entirely qualified for a position in your company, ask yourself these very important questions: Are they more qualified than any other candidate? Are you sure that their relation to you isn't part of that qualification? Is it entirely based on skills and relative experience? If you still want to tell yourself that you are being objective about this decision, then continue on, but tread lightly.

Regardless of your self-perceived objectivity, your staff will most likely not feel the same. And no matter how skilled your family member or friend is, they will have to work overtime to prove themselves to a staff that suspects favoritism and nepotism. This scenario isn't fair to anyone involved, isn't worth the feel-good that you will temporarily receive, and in all likelihood will end up being an embarrassing blip on the employee's résumé.

CHAPTER 4

WE LOVE YOU, YOU'RE HIRED

Sent: July 25, 11:30 p.m.
From: CEO
To: Executive Team
Subject: Jim's Interview

Hi, everyone. Thanks for taking the time to interview Jim McDonald this afternoon. He comes highly recommended by our board for the VP of sales position. I know he's the first and only candidate we've interviewed, but let's fast-track the feedback loop. We need to get our numbers back up by the end of Q3. Reply all and let me know what you thought of him!

Reply All From: Suzanne, Dir. of Operations
To: Executive Team
Subject: Jim's Interview

I thought he was great! Very high on the likability index!

Reply All From: Bob, Dir. of Product Strategy
To: Executive Team
Subject: Jim's Interview

Small world. Turns out he used to work at the same company as my brother. They were in different departments though. Seems like a nice guy.

Reply All From: Carol, Dir. of Customer Experience
To: Executive Team
Subject: Jim's Interview

He's funny! I bet our customers would love him.

Reply All From: Jane, Dir. of Technology
To: Executive Team
Subject: Jim's Interview

He's fine. I won't really interact with him, so I don't care. Just please make sure he's not a technical troglodyte. I don't have time to babysit the sales guy's laptop problems.

Reply All From: Diane, Dir. of Marketing
To: Executive Team
Subject: Jim's Interview

He'd make a great travel partner for my upcoming trade shows—seems like a lot of fun. Great culture fit!

Reply All From: Joe, Associate VP of Sales
To: Executive Team
Subject: Jim's Interview

I don't really know what I'm supposed to be working on right now, so yeah, it would be great if I could have a manager sooner rather than later. When can he start?

When you've got an open position as important as a revenue-generating position like VP of Sales, get a butt in that seat ASAP! There's no time to waste. Every minute that position isn't filled, there is money falling through the hole in the bottom of the boat and the boat is taking on water quickly.

Don't waste time or money with recruiters or headhunters. When someone as important as your Founder or your Board refers a candidate, consider it a slam dunk! Get that person in for an interview loop right away with your senior-most people and fast-track the feedback loop. Being accepted and liked by your senior team is the most important qualification—you can fill in the skill gaps later. Like they say, hire for culture first, skills second. If he's well liked, your team will be more apt to do his job for him so he's successful and won't cause unnecessary performance pressure on the rest of the team.

The fact that your Founder or your Board doesn't really understand the requirements of the position is beside the point. They know what's best and will be flattered if you hire one of their referrals without question. If things go poorly down the road, you can blame them.

LET'S GET REAL

Reply All From: Sue, Director of Human Resources
To: Executive Team
Subject: Jim's Interview

DID ANYONE ASK HIM IF HE CAN SELL? Just curious.

"Hire slow, fire fast" is one of the most important mantras of good team-building. A deliberate, thoughtful, and strategic hiring process is the best investment you can make in your company. Yes, while hiring to values and culture is incredibly important, don't forget that you are hiring people for their skills and their ability to get the job done and add value to the business.

All too often, interview loops and hiring procedures are so rushed and informal that candidates aren't vetted for skills at all. They are assessed for their likability and "fit," and because they were referred from a credible source or "look good on paper," the assumption is made that they can do the job. Here are a few tips and tricks to make sure you get the proof before you make the hire:

1. **Invest in professional recruiting.** It is always worth the money to hire a reputable professional recruiter or headhunter for senior hires. Negotiate a smart deal, and make sure they are financially motivated to guarantee that your new hire is successful. They'll ensure that you vet multiple candidates, help you avoid the temptation to move too fast, and run a fair process.

2. **Talk to referrals. Really talk to referrals.** Never think of checking referrals as "checking a box" in the recruiting process. Try to have thoughtful conversations, ask unexpected questions, and consider looking for hints and clues in their answers.

3. **Do background research via networking.** Find out where this person stands in your industry, what their reputation is—and, yes, dig into their LinkedIn profiles and Google them. Take the time to find out as much as you can about both their character and their skills. Make professional background checks a standard policy

for every new hire, it's easy to outsource, affordable, and worth it.

4. **Require specific proof-points.** Don't be shy about asking for work samples (writing samples, presentations, videos, proposals, etc.) that back up the candidate's claims.

It is far better to have a vacancy than a bad fit. Some say the cost of a bad hire is the equivalent of three times that person's annual salary. From disruption to the organization, to bad PR, to a "do-over" in the hiring process, a rushed or bad hire can be incredibly costly. Take the time to do it right; insist that your interviewers take the process seriously, ask smart questions, and deliver thoughtful feedback to you.

If the open position is a management position, you may decide to include their potential subordinates in the vetting process. Should you do so, make sure they understand that they are not part of the decision-making process, but that their opinions are valuable by giving them something specific to probe for or score against. Having subordinates focus on a values fit is an excellent way to include them in the process.

Never hesitate to bring candidates in for a second round, and certainly don't feel like you've wasted their time by doing so. A smart, great-fit hire is as valuable to them as it is to you. So beware the impatient candidate; they should share your desire to take all the time that's needed to make sure it's a win-win for everyone. Even if you've narrowed the field to a single candidate, multiple rounds of interviews are expected and accepted by most job-seekers.

CHAPTER 5

DAY ONE DILEMMA

FIRST DAY AT LARGE TECHNOLOGY COMPANY IN REDMOND, WASHINGTON:

Nancy had just started her new position as a mid-level executive in the marketing division at Large Technology Company after going through a two-month recruiting and interviewing process. She interviewed with over ten different people and went through multiple rounds of testing. It was the most difficult process she had ever experienced in her career, but it resulted in an offer for her dream job at her dream company. She felt it was worth the canine obstacle course she'd had to go through to get the job. It's everything she wanted; she was thrilled!

The night before she was to start, she received an email from her new boss informing her that he would be out of town for two weeks and that the team would be taking care of her. This added a certain level of stress to her first day, but after the interviewing process she felt as if she had earned her place on the team, and it didn't overly concern her. However, it did add an element of doubt to her ability to be successful.

Upon arrival, there was no one to greet her, several empty cubicles in the section she was supposed to be in, and no direction, orientation, or any other indication as to what she should be doing. As a resourceful person, she started asking around among her fellow teammates. The most popular answers were "I don't know," "not sure," "call HR," "wait till John gets back," and even a "who are you?" None of these filled her with confidence that she had made the right decision to come to work at this company.

She attempted to get a hold of HR, but was shuffled around multiple times. She was vaguely sure she had the right cube identified. When the manager had previously met with her for the offer, he had gestured in the general direction of that cube. Day one was spent setting up the cube with things she would need—or what she thought she would need. Day two was much the same, and by day three HR had been in touch and helped set up her email account, but she still had no computer. Remember, this was one of the tech behemoths. She was getting anxious.

By day five she had managed to get in touch with IT and got a computer, but now didn't know what she was supposed to do with it. She decided to interview her teammates to find out what they were working on and what they thought she should be working on. The following week she did more of the same and started familiarizing herself with the various software platforms and brand guidelines for the partners—with very little help or input from her team. They were treating her like an interloper and made her feel like she didn't belong. She was wishing she had taken the other offer.

Finally, after two weeks, John returned from vacation and asked what she had been up to. In a nonjudgmental way, she tried to explain that she was a little surprised by the lack of direction, orientation, and collaboration from the team. John just smiled and said, "Welcome to the team. Sounds like it went as it should have!"

What she now knew was that if she were to succeed, it would always be on her own. Full stop.

MEMO TO FILE FROM JOHN:

New employee started two weeks ago; sounds like everything went great. It was unfortunate that I had to take that trip to Bermuda at the last minute, but how could I say no to my buddies? She was resourceful and figured things out—exactly as I planned it, even if I hadn't had to take that personal trip! She got the purposeful cold shoulder from the team because she might be taking one of their jobs one day. And they pretty much hazed her like they all were hazed on their first weeks on the job. Survival of the fittest and all that. If more companies would take this approach, we wouldn't have such needy and dependent employees.

They need to learn how to be independent and stand up for themselves. No free lunches here. None of the BS about touchy-feely onboarding—that is strictly for wimps. Not the warrior workplace I love and thrive in. If one of your own gets eaten now and then, so be it; only the strong survive. A little natural selection is a good thing when building a solid team. (Note to self: Keep this for upcoming book on CrossFit Leadership.)

LET'S GET REAL

This is NOT how you onboard someone. They've just spent weeks or months going through interviews, stressing, preparing and then making a choice to come work for you. They are probably leaving another job and possibly choosing between multiple offers. They start off so hopeful. Why would you want to ruin that on day one by purposely not reinforcing that they've just made a great decision to come work for you?

Make day one count. Don't have them fill out forms for the day or, as our example above, ignore them. Celebrate that they made the right decision; show them you're excited that they are here. Have all their equipment and paperwork ready on their first day so they can be productive. Take them out to lunch or have a team lunch to reinforce their welcome by the company. Based on your company's values, have others share why this company is a good place to work. Take them around and introduce them to their team members or as many people as possible.

The last thing you want is them going home and telling their partner or family that it was the worst first day and they think they may have made a mistake. Or worse, they don't want to go back for day two.

When someone leaves—assuming it's a retirement or a promotion to another position or company—we usually give them a heartfelt goodbye-and-good-luck party. We celebrate who they are and their contribution to the company. Why shouldn't we start out this way as well?

Think about your kid's first day of school: if the teacher spends most of his or her time demonstrating to the kids that it's going to be fun, they are going to be accepted, they are going to like it, and will want to return. The first day of a new job should be no different.

CHAPTER 6

TANNED, TONED, AND TIGHT BEFORE TALENT

CEO: Gina, I'm so excited—I've found the perfect person for our new PR manager! I want you to meet her as soon as possible because I want to make an offer tomorrow. Can you make some time to meet with her today?

HR Manager: Wait a minute, who is this person? I don't recall seeing her résumé.

CEO: She doesn't have one; I met her, and it was like love at first sight. She is absolutely wonderful and has the look I want for the role.

HR Manager: Look? What are you talking about? The job description clearly states we need someone with five years of experience in running an agency team and who has handled multiple crisis situations. What does that have to do with looks?

CEO: Oh my lord, can't you ever just think out of the box? You are so literal sometimes; it's really frustrating when I'm trying to recruit the best talent. Can't you just let go of your requirements and trust my instincts when I tell you this person is amazing?

HR Manager: I'm not saying this person isn't the right person for the job; I'm only trying to avoid another mis-hire, like we've had in the past when we've looked past someone's résumé. It's never gone well for us. Remember John? You loved his charisma and so-called wit, and you said not to worry about a background check, but his résumé turned out to be total fiction. Remember we lost one of our best customers because he slept with their representative and promised all sorts of things we couldn't deliver? He didn't even know how the basic products worked! And he did not have a degree! Which, by the way, was a job requirement, so thank God none of the other applicants we didn't hire found out, or we could have been sued. And why doesn't she have a résumé?

CEO: God, you are such a stick-in-the-mud. For a creative agency, I don't know how we ended up with you. What are you, the people police? Listen, don't remind me about John. I was so pissed and hurt when I found out about his sleeping with that rep; you have no clue what a betrayal that was to me. Anyway, I have great instincts when it comes to hiring; I can just look at someone and know they are the right fit by how they look. I'm surprised you can't do that as the HR manager. Isn't that a requirement for your job?

HR Manager: Looks are not everything. Now, tell me why she doesn't have a résumé.

CEO: She's just starting out in her career, and she's a free spirit, so she doesn't want to be defined by labels. I love that! She's got this amazing full-arm tattoo sleeve that just screams credibility for a cool agency look. Can't you just imagine what people will say when they see her as the face of the company? She's got the look!

HR Manager: I don't know how a tattoo sleeve is relevant for someone who not only needs to be able to speak to our brand and make sure we are seen but also manage us through a crisis. We have no policy and don't care about tattoos, but seriously, does she have any experience whatsoever?

CEO: Look, she doesn't have a résumé, and I told her she didn't need one. I found her at the Starbucks I go to, because I admired her tattoo, her piercings, and her "out there" attitude. She just fits the part! Almost like she came right out of casting after I imagined what this person should look like!

HR Manager: OK, so let me be clear. She has no relevant work experience whatsoever, she has none of the skills on the job description, but you liked how she looked and that she made a good caramel macchiato and had a bit of attitude. Is that about the gist of it?

CEO: Yes. Obviously, when you put it like that, it doesn't sound as good as it did in my head, but I don't care. She is perfect, and I want to make her an offer.

HR Manager: So do you even need me to interview her, or is it a forgone conclusion that our new PR manager is your tattooed barista?

CEO: Since you are being completely obtuse about this, let's just make her the offer. Write it up and get it out to her today.

CEO leans back in his chair with an "I can't believe some people" look on his face and says to an imaginary camera: When making a hiring decision, the most important aspect is always how the person presents themselves to you. You have to be brave and willing to hire on sheer guts based on looks because, ultimately, who moves up in the world? Those that look the part. We can train for the rest, but I want someone who is the face of our brand, because that's what someone will see first.

It's our first impression, and the most lasting one. Don't let a cranky HR manager tell you otherwise. It's first and foremost about how they look and what brand they show up with. Trust your instincts!

LET'S GET REAL

The most successful hiring takes into account how someone presents themselves to the world, but it's only one piece of the puzzle, and it's definitely not about beauty or fashion. Professional experience, skills, and real-world proof that they will add value to the organization trumps everything. But unless coupled with good presentation, oral skills, language use, social skills, and yes, professional appearance suitable for your business or industry are there, the skills may never make it into practice. We get taken in or put off by someone's looks. Remember to dig deeper in both cases. One's résumé matters, experience matters, natural talent matters, and cultural fit and values matter. Take a look at the job description that is the basis of the job. How likely is it that the person has what it takes to be successful? Usually, none of this shows on the surface.

Don't let yourself be dazzled by someone's sparkle until you determine if it's a diamond or a cubic zirconia. The fakes will cost you money, time, and reputation.

CHAPTER 7

RED STAPLERS

Sent: September 17, 8:00 a.m.
From: Diana, Director of Human Resources
To: Joe, Founder & CEO
Subject: Sam

Joe,

I know you think the world of Sam, and he's been with the company for going on twenty years, but this is literally the fourteenth position that he's held with the company in that time frame. His record is that he has not been able to stay in any one position for more than six months. He either fails miserably at the task at hand, is rejected en masse by his co-workers and team members, or develops a horrendous attendance problem.

Can we at long last please terminate him for nonperformance?

Sincerely concerned,

Diana

Sent: September 17, 8:05 a.m.
From: Joe, Founder & CEO
To: Diana, Director of Human Resources
Subject: Sam

Diana,

Absolutely not. Sam was one of my first hires and has been with me through thick and thin. I'll never fire him—ever—and neither will you. Just find something for him to do.

Don't ask me again.

Joe

By all means! You owe it to your most loyal employees to give them every opportunity to fail, and when they do they deserve a second chance—and a third, and a fourth. Long-term and well-liked employees are every bit as important as the high performers. You can't have all high-performing employees, right? And the hanger-on-ers put things into perspective and help the top performers feel more valuable. It is better to have a few hanger-on-ers than to be the bad guy by firing them. So, yes, make it clear to your HR team that their job is to move these people from job to job as often as possible, make them feel successful, and convince the rest of the staff that their new position is mission critical to the company's success.

A skilled HR professional can easily create job titles and descriptions that sound important but really have no deliverables or outputs. Consider job titles such as Assistant Researcher, Information Specialist, or Director of Company Archives. If your hanger-on-er is the well-liked social type, consider a more modern title, such as Culture Czar, People Person, or Corporate Event Specialist. Even the most incompetent professional can appear to succeed in these jobs for at least six months.

If your hanger-on-er is struggling, even with the vaguest of job titles, consider a lengthy training regimen. Oftentimes, a senior hanger-on-er can appear successful by completing a company-sponsored online MBA program. "Jim is working part-time as he's getting his MBA" is a great cover-up. Who knows, Jim might actually get smarter through this process, but even if he doesn't, it buys you two more years of not having to fire him.

"Out of sight, out of mind" theory also works to alleviate some of the friction this might cause with the rest of the staff, so consider having these folks work from home. This is a sure-fire way of maintaining some mystery around them and their contribution to the company. Your staff will see them on the org chart, meet them once or twice a year at the company holiday party or summer picnic, and you can continue the charade that they are integral employees while also forever avoiding the dreaded firing that will make you feel bad about yourself.

You can't be an effective leader if you feel guilty about every little thing, and certainly about every single person. You also can't run the risk of a negative GlassDoor review from a disgruntled employee or a wrongful termination suit from a litigious employee. So pay the price of avoiding risk, and send them to the basement!

LET'S GET REAL

There are few things more unfair in employment practices than keeping someone in a job that they are not qualified for or, worse, just not performing. As a leader and hiring manager, *it is your job* to have a constant eye on whether or not each and every member of your team is in a role that is a good fit, and an integral part of the company's success. No one should ever be put in or left in a position simply to reciprocate loyalty or due to your fear of confrontation and bad feelings.

It is human nature to want to feel like a contributor and be successful, but for some people, that can be overcome by a fear of change. People stay in jobs they aren't qualified for all the time, and some will stay as long as you allow them to, simply because they are afraid of not having a job at all or fear making a life change.

It is also human nature to want to be on a team where everyone is pulling their weight. Don't think for a second that the non-contributing, non-performing employee that you are hiding in your organization because of your own guilt isn't resented by your high-performing employees. Everyone in your organization knows about the guy with the red stapler in the basement, and this is unfair to everyone involved and makes you look like an enabling parent.

To avoid hanger-on-er syndrome, consider creating a rigorous 30/60/90-day plan for all new employees. Build in checkpoints to make sure they are guided and directed toward success (see Chapter 3 to avoid the Day One Dilemma and create a thoughtful onboarding process). At ninety days, if your employee has not proven that they are on the path to success, cut bait and let them go. This is how to execute the "hire slow, fire fast" mantra. Give them ample runway, but set them free if it's not going to work out. And face it: you'll know. The question is whether or not you're going to be in denial about it.

Strong leaders are in touch with their employees' satisfaction, happiness, and motivations for work. And strong leaders are decisive and brave enough to make tough decisions when employees are unable to make them for themselves.

CHAPTER 8

PERFORMANCE REVIEWS FOR DUMMIES

Sent: September 5, 9:05 a.m.
From: Ken, VP of Sales
To: Barb, Sales Associate
Subject: Your Performance Review

Hey Barb,

Sorry I'm going to be late to our meeting; I'm desperate for a coffee. Back in about ten. Text me if you want one. If 9:30 doesn't work for you, let me know; it's totally no big deal at all. We don't even really have to meet about your review. You're doing a good job; keep up the great work.

Ken

P.S. We're not doing pay raises until the end of the second quarter, that I know of. I'll let you know if I hear differently.

Performance reviews are passé, overrated, and a complete waste of your valuable time. As every good leader knows, if your people don't know where they stand without you having to take the time to tell them or write it down in plain English, then they probably shouldn't be working for you. In the event that your HR director *insists* that you personally administer a performance review—especially for your most valuable senior management team—let's make sure you start off by setting the record straight: *This is not about them.* It's a painful inconvenience for you that you do not enjoy.

The following are some general rules of thumb to ensure that your team will dread performance reviews as much as you do:

1. Schedule your performance reviews for no more than fifteen minutes. This is all the time it should take to tell your employees that they are underperforming and need to step up or step out. As the appointment approaches, make sure you either (a) do not show up or (b) reschedule *at least twice* at the last minute. This will send a clear message that this process is not a priority for you, and neither are they.

2. If and when the meeting does finally occur, make sure you start with the bad news by informing them that they did not meet the goals you had in mind. Yes, these are different than the goals written in their last performance review, but as the manager, you changed them midstream to better align with your vision, which is your prerogative. Notifying them of the revised goals isn't necessary. Top people should know when you've changed your mind.

3. Performance reviews are an excellent opportunity to restate your authority, so make sure you do all the talking. Talking over your employees will give them the opportunity to think hard about what they need to do to make you happy. However, do take a moment in between thoughts to check your phone. Important text messages cannot wait, and your employees will understand that you have much more pressing matters than criticizing their idiosyncrasies.

4. Lastly, and perhaps most importantly, be open and prepared for emotional outbursts. Crying is a natural reaction to a well-crafted and masterfully delivered performance review, and you should be proud when you achieve this breakthrough with any employee.

By following these four basic rules of thumb, you can be sure the performance review was administered in a way that will foster fear among your staff and become a hallmark of your leadership for years to come. Remember, the more your employees dread their performance reviews, the better. It will ensure that they put on a top-notch performance at least a few weeks out of the year, right before review (bonus) time.

LET'S GET REAL

Yes, "traditional" performance reviews are being replaced by 360-degree assessments and daily feedback cycles, and HR professionals are experimenting with all kinds of systems and platforms for constructive feedback. But one thing is for sure: as CEO or a leader, there is no better way to spend your time than having honest, thoughtful, and constructive conversations with your team about your expectations and their performance. Never assume someone knows how they are doing. **It's not up to them to know, it's up to you to make sure they know.**

Generally speaking, managers dread administering performance reviews because (a) they have not been an effective manager in the day-to-day, and the performance review is going to include delivering some sort of unexpected news or (b) the platform or system for the review is too cumbersome or complicated to be effective.

No performance review can take the place of good people-management and communication along the way. Employees should know where they stand at all times and should be communicated with about the progress against their goals daily. Their jobs should be designed so that they align with their goals—if they are doing the job, they are achieving the goals. Lofty goals set once a year that are dissociated from the day-to-day tasks of the job will only be out of sight and out of mind.

Be wary of managers who complain loudly that HR isn't involved enough in performance management, or that a new performance-management platform or software is needed. Again, performance management is really about how well the job description and tasks are aligned with the goals of the individual and how well those goals are aligned with the company goals. If you don't have that figured out as a leadership team, no software program will figure it out for you.

Why do employees care about employee reviews, assuming performance and goal achievement have been addressed along the way? The answer: promotions and compensation. Make sure your promotion and compensation philosophies are well crafted, well communicated, and, most of all, consistent throughout the organization. There should be zero exceptions to these policies. If your employees know what their goals are, their jobs are designed to meet those goals, and they understand exactly how they will be rewarded for meeting those goals, the rest is smooth sailing.

Remember, your people are the central nervous system of your business. If they aren't being managed effectively, or if their satisfaction and happiness aren't top priorities, then it will wreak havoc in every other aspect of your business.

SECTION 2

GETTING IT TOGETHER

Team dynamics are complicated and often messy. It takes good leadership to bring out the best in each and every team member and recognize the team effort versus the effort of the leader. However, it's not about the leader; it's about the team, and the two become inextricable in great teams.

Great teams accomplish amazing things, and that requires both the team members and the leaders to cede control for individual accomplishment in service of the team. Those teams whose members need individual recognition ultimately fail, as do those that make it all about the leader. Think of great orchestra conductors. They stand in front of the orchestra and wave a baton. They play no instrument and have no audible contribution to the music, but when done well, the results are breathtaking. They know how and when to bring out the individual contributions in service of the team—the greater good—and the result the team can produce. Only through this team effort is beautiful music played and heard.

When famous conductors go off the rails it's usually because they fail to value the team above themselves. It becomes about them, their idiosyncrasies, and not the joint contribution of the team. This is usually because the leader has let the big "E" word take over: Ego. When ego creeps into the picture, the production of the team—whatever that may be—is always less than it could have been. In some circles, big egos are allowed, even encouraged. However, you will always see a reduction in the performance of the team because it is no longer balanced. Everyone else on the team is a sidekick to the egocentric leader or the star player. Individual contributions that are not simply part of the team production stand outside the circle and detract from performance.

Leading a great team is like walking a tightrope in the beginning: lose your balance and you're on the ground. If there is no safety net and you were pretty high up, this is particularly painful. Look at any of the great sports teams that continue to win, year after year. It's about the team, not individual players. Each can be celebrated for their contribution, but without the others, they are nothing more than a great individual contributor. Getting your balance as the leader of a team means being more aware of your team members' contributions than your own.

Organizations are no different than orchestras or sports teams. It takes the precise performance of everyone at the right time to make a strategy come together. Any one person taking credit, hoarding, blaming, or shaming will break apart a team faster than church letting out before a big meal. Results will happen; just not what you originally intended.

Great leaders make sure the team crosses the finish line together—with the leader bringing up the rear.

CHAPTER 9

PISSED-OFF POSSE

Sent: March 5, 6:00 a.m.
From: Cindy, CEO
To: Karen, Chief Strategy Officer; Steve, Chief Operations Officer
Subject: Leveling the Playing Field

Steve and Karen,

Good morning, you two. Hey, so I have been thinking about next week's strategic planning session. I know you both have strong opinions about the agenda and what you want to accomplish in the session. I'd like to hear them. You two are the only ones that I'd ever confess this to, but I've never led a strategic planning session. In fact, I've never even really been to one at this level. Kinda leaves you wondering how I got to be CEO without having that experience under my belt, but I did. Call it luck, I guess! So yeah, maybe you guys could give me some guidance here.

I want to show up as a leader, though, so maybe we can meet privately and you guys can give me your ideas. Then, during the breaks in the meeting, we can chat out of earshot of the rest of the team and you can let me know if I'm doing OK. You guys are so great—it's so great to have so much support. This is a big job, being the CEO, and I couldn't do it without you, for sure. You both have so much more experience than I do with developing strategic plans, but I'm more of a people person. We make a great team! It's kind of like we all just report to each other, isn't it? This is going to be a great planning session! Looking forward to hearing the ideas you have for me.

Cindy

Sent: March 5, 6:05 a.m.
From: Karen
To: Steve
Subject: RE: Leveling the Playing Field

Steve, WTF is this? Is she really this stupid and clueless? I mean, I know she's new to the CEO role here at JobSpots, but how on earth did she get this gig and what planet did she come from? I have been under the impression that she was coming in with some big vision. Guess not, eh?

Karen

Sent: March 5, 6:15 a.m.
From: Steve
To: Karen
Subject: RE: RE: Leveling the Playing Field

Karen, WTF x2. I have no idea, and there is no way in hell I'm going to be her handler and the ghost writer of her "brilliant strategic ideas." Is she kidding us with this? Who does she think we are? This is not how I roll. Plus, I have an entire operational infrastructure proposal to present to the board.

Steve

Sent: March 5, 6:21 a.m.
From: Karen
To: Steve
Subject: RE: RE: RE: Leveling the Playing Field

Yeah, not to mention the board asked me for a product roadmap. That IS my job after all. Since when do you and I have to be shadow CEO and do our day jobs? If she thinks we'd be a better CEO than she is, then why don't we just suggest THAT to the board!!!???

Karen

Sent: March 5, 6:24 a.m.
From: Steve
To: Karen
Subject: RE: RE: RE: RE: Leveling the Playing Field

Hey, so this reminds me, have you talked to Jim over at CareerHut lately? I guess he's moving on to start his own business, buying a winery or something. It's going to leave an executive vacancy at our biggest competitor. You could totally do that job. I could do that job.

Steve

Sent: March 5, 6:28 a.m.
From: Karen
To: Steve
Subject: RE: RE: RE: RE: RE: Leveling the Playing Field

Steve, you're a genius. It's a much bigger company than JobSpots, you know. If we BOTH went there, we could blow her out of the water. And without us here, she'd be the Empress with No Clothes. The whole thing would go down in flames in a week.

Karen

Sent: March 5, 6:29 a.m.
From: Steve
To: Karen

Subject: RE: RE: RE: RE: RE: RE: Leveling the Playing Field

That'd level the playing field, all right.

Steve

Sent: March 5, 6:30 a.m.
From: Karen
To: Steve
Subject: RE: RE: RE: RE: RE: RE: RE: Leveling the Playing Field

We'd better use our personal emails for this conversation.

Karen

And in a matter of thirty minutes, early on a Tuesday morning, a plan was hatched.

LET'S GET REAL

Let's talk about imposter syndrome. Odds are you are going to have some degree of it. Most leaders who aren't narcissists do. It's perfectly natural to rise to a level in your career that makes you feel a little unsure, shakes your confidence, or even makes you feel like you're not worthy of the stature and authority—or even pay grade—that you have achieved. But many leaders lean too heavily on the talents and experiences of those around them to shore up their lack of confidence, rather than doing the work necessary to build their own.

Talented senior managers will fill every void they see in the interest of their own goals and the goals of the business. If that void is you, then you can rest assured that someone will either oust you from below or fly right over you without you ever seeing it coming. They will also have spotted a weakness in your leadership, which is especially useful information for when they go to work for your competitor!

Again, to be fair, it is perfectly normal to be unsure of yourself, and it is even sometimes OK to be out of your depth in experience and skill. But get the help you need from the right resources. There are leadership coaches, CEO coaches, leadership peer groups, or even some board members who will be a good fit for mentoring you and sharpening your skills.

Like it or not, you are the captain, and your crew—no matter how capable or how experienced—is counting on you to act like one.

CHAPTER 10

TEAM-BUILDING FOR TODDLERS

Sent: August 8
From: CEO
To: Extended Management Team
Subject: Leadership Retreat

To all,

I'm very excited to share the agenda for our leadership retreat coming up in two weeks. First of all, our destination is a total score! We were able to schedule this year's retreat at Haley's Dude Ranch in Idaho, which will be great to take us all back to our cowboy roots! Can't wait to get into my boots and feel the horse between my legs. For those of you who have not ridden before, get on board because you'll all be doing it—it's a requirement!

Everyone should be prepared to bring rough-and-ready clothes, jeans, shorts, and boots or whatever you feel comfortable wearing. Just remember that we'll be getting up close and personal.

The consultant we've hired has crafted an amazing agenda for all of us. We'll start off by doing our usual "trust fall" exercise. Be sure to pick a partner that you haven't done this with before. If you can't trust your teammates to catch you, how can we be successful as a team?

We'll be doing more than one, and after the first one your partner will be chosen at random, so be ready for a few falls!

Then we have a great exercise in the barn: You'll all be stuck in a dirty horse stall and partnered up with a couple of your peers. Your job will be to clean it up with whatever you find in the stall, and the door won't open till you're done! Should be a lot of fun! Be sure to bring clothes you don't mind getting dirty because there will be no avoiding the filth! Our version of a little reality show!

Then it's off to the horses. You'll all be charged with taking your horse on the full trail ride, and no dinner till you get back. We will have a few guides to help us along the way, but don't count on them for much as this will be more of a survival exercise than a feel-good excursion.

That evening we'll have our usual dinner roast with everyone sharing the most embarrassing story about themselves—the funnier the better! And feel free to share one about your peers too. Remember, raunchy stories are good stories. HR will be nowhere in sight for this one! We'll be sure to bring the anatomically correct blow-up sheep we had last year, just in case anyone needs inspiration for some fun!

The following morning we'll have our regular business meeting, and each of you will be invited (required) to share your most memorable lesson learned from the previous day. We might get to the strategic planning if we have time.

The whole point of the retreat is to bond and develop a level of trust that will take the team to new heights of success. Bring your true, authentic self, and let it all hang out. You will be judged on how well you're able to let your hair down and be real.

What happens at the retreat stays at the retreat! (Until it doesn't—remember Pete from last year?? I'll never forget when his wife found out about it at the holiday party!)

See you all there!

Chris

Take a lesson from Chris, CEO of cutting loose:

> *I always believe in inspiring the team with these free-for-all retreats. No bullshit exercises built for toddlers here; these are bonding exercises for adults. And we need to start acting like adults—who knows what will happen when everyone is forced to reveal their secrets! It's always been great, although lately we usually lose someone.*
>
> *But hey, survival of the fittest. Last year, more people than I expected came down with the flu right before the retreat. I certainly hope that doesn't happen this year. I've noted who those folks are.*
>
> *The board was on me to explain what results I was hoping to get by spending all the money on this retreat, but I simply told them that teams that play together stay together, and they bought it. Really, I just want a getaway that let's everyone cut loose without all the damn HR rules and regulations on us. Everyone always has a great time, and if it doesn't really accomplish a business purpose, who cares? We are bonding and forming tighter relationships, so it's all good.*

LET'S GET REAL

Team-building has gotten a bad rap over the years because the "purpose" is generally ill-defined and/or has nothing to do with the actual activities. Our CEO, Chris, is designing a retreat that is bound to fail and could result in lawsuits because of so many over-the-line requirements or suggestions that are really directives.

Go back to basics. Why is it good to cultivate the team? Because they work better when they get along and respect one another. Encouraging a sense of belonging is a good thing and increases overall employee satisfaction. However, how you do this will depend on several factors: What are your values? What are you trying to achieve? Do you have some team issues? A new program you're trying to brainstorm? A strategic plan that has stalled? Whatever the reason, figure it out beforehand and design an agenda that supports that purpose.

Once defined, it's important to make it overt, not covert. State what you are trying to achieve, and ask everyone to help you achieve that. That's the *team* in teamwork—it's not solely up to you. They may likely have better ideas than you, so let them chime in. Incorporate fun things that have nothing to do with work, but make them optional. Not everyone is comfortable with what we deem fun or interesting.

It's important to have options because males and females, or people of different ethnicities or faiths, may not think everything on the list is appropriate for them, but you don't want them to feel excluded. Going to a *dude* ranch may not feel great for women, telling embarrassing stories could cross the line into harassment, and anatomically correct blow-up animals are just plain wrong in any work setting. Even when you are not on company premises, the rules of the company still apply. As do those of common sense and decency.

Team-building should be happening every day in the workplace—encouraging good behavior, recognizing contributions, and guiding others to success. Great teams lead naturally and inject fun and comradery into everyday interactions. It doesn't need to be an artificially staged event that most adults will think is childish. Encouraging people to stretch beyond what they think they can do is one thing; forcing them to participate in childish and pointless rituals is completely inappropriate.

CHAPTER 11

FRAT HOUSE FRENZY

Sent: October 1
From: Scott, CEO
To: All Employees
Subject: Business Travel Rules

Hey guys,

Just want to clarify a few things—btw, I know you're not all guys and I should probably change that greeting, but hey, I built this company and I'm not going to change now!

The title of this email is "Business Travel Rules"—which, when I read that, I crack myself up because business travel really does rule!! But unfortunately, that's not what this is about.

I got a big old hand slap from Ms. HR herself, Hannah, about some of the free-forming norms that we use when traveling. First, get things approved before you go, OK? I know, this should be basic, but some of "us" aren't doing it, so pretty please?

Second, regarding the drinks, reign it in a little, guys!! Even I can't have six tequila shots both before and after dinner! Kudos to whoever tried to pass that expense report in, and whoa, keep it up, dude, just not on our dime, OK? According to Hannah, we need to start listing the purpose for all of the expenses, including the meals, and "to meet ho's" apparently is not appropriate (although pretty funny!).

Apparently, we do have an employee handbook, and we all need to read it and sign it as I guess there is some good stuff in there to help keep us from getting sued. Get that in to Hannah Banana as soon as you can. She'll explain anything you don't understand. We've got a few unhappy campers here—especially the women—so we need to see what we can do to make the ladies happy!

Here's the big bummer: we can't have booze in the office anymore. I guess we're being sued by someone who joined one of our after-parties. Not even sure who brought him into the building, but he drove drunk and hit a bunch of parked cars, so his insurance is suing us—and so are some of the owners of the trashed cars. Oh yeah, we can't have unescorted guests here anymore as well. They all need to pass through the security downstairs. Really sorry about that. I will miss some of our "guests" at the after-work parties!

Oh yeah, we've gone through three cleaning companies in the last two months as they refuse to clean up after our parties, and apparently, we now have a mouse problem because of all the food in the cubes. Clean up after yourselves, guys. Remember, yo' mama doesn't work here—at least I don't think so! Ha!

OK, I think those were all the things I was mandated to say, but hey, it's all good.

Sent: October 2
From: Hannah
To: All Employees
Subject: Email from CEO re Business Travel Rules

All Employees:

The board of directors has asked me to follow up on Scott's email from yesterday regarding our handbooks and business travel rules. Scott is on indefinite sabbatical and Ron, the chairman, will be filling in for him until his return.

Please disregard any suggestive or inappropriate wording in his email. The board would like me to inform you that it does not reflect the values of the company.

You will all be required to sign the employee handbook after reading it by 5:00 p.m. today. If you are out of the office today, you will be required to read and sign it before returning to work.

You will all be required to follow all business travel rules in the future, or you will not be reimbursed. You might also be subject to discipline or termination, based on the policies in our handbook.

Please keep your cubicle clean or, again, you may be subject to discipline according to our new policy, outlined in the handbook.

Lastly, my name is not Hannah Banana and do not address me as such.

Sincerely,

HR

LET'S GET REAL

Yes, this may have seemed extreme, but again, it's a real example. Some leaders never grow up and want to relive their "fun times" in the workplace, much to the dismay of the employees. Although there will always be some who love it, it doesn't help productivity and it opens you up to all sorts of potential legal trouble.

A good test for determining if you should behave a certain way or implement a specific policy in the workplace is whether or not you could or would want to credibly defend it on network news. We used to say, "Would you like this to be your *60 Minutes* moment?" Most of those guys are so old they wouldn't recognize the workplace of today anyway! So, think network news: Do you want to have to defend a policy that allows drunken parties and illicit behavior? Never say or do what you can't defend.

The workplace isn't your college dorm; it's not your church; it's not a comedy club; it's not a fun house or a ballpark. It's a place of work. It's up to you, as the leader, to make it conducive to the day-to-day business—not a place to play. This often seems to be forgotten in the need to attract and retain top talent. It's OK if we bend the rules a little; it will make people happy, and happy employees are productive employees, right? Yes, BUT— that's a big *but*—you have to stay in the lanes.

There is just so much that can go wrong when you mix work, alcohol, or drugs—any kind of behavior that should only be done on personal time. You want to protect the company and your employees. You are not running an adult day-care center. If you are, plan on lots of legal bills and frustrations because your liability just went up exponentially.

Provide a safe place for people to work; encourage friendships to form, but limit what happens on work time. If you don't want your employees to be romantically involved with each other, define it. If you're OK with that, define it. Either way is acceptable as long as you put up the guardrails to protect everyone. Think of yourself as a risk manager. Your people can be one of your biggest areas of risk. Help them stay safe, feel productive, and feel like they belong, and they'll help the company succeed.

CHAPTER 12

GRADING ON THE CURVE

Sent: August 8
From: CEO
To: Department Heads
Subject: Stack-Ranking Deliverable

Department Heads,

I want to see all of your rankings for your employees in my inbox by Friday. I know you all disagree with my methodology; however, it's not up to you. I've listened to your arguments and concluded that I was right in the first place. So please adhere to the following procedure:

1. Evaluate all of your employees with a score of 1–10 based on the following:

    a. Timeliness

    b. Neatness

    c. Ability to be an independent worker (doesn't ask too many questions)

    d. Quantity of work performed on a scale of 1–10 (10 being the highest)

> e. Quality of work performed (how many times do you have to correct them?)
>
> f. Overall ability to fit into the team
>
> g. Cultural fit

8. Take their total score and divide it by seven to get their average, and then do the same for the entire team to get your team average.

9. The people above the average will get raises; the people below will not.

10. Then send your data to HR, and he will compile the "team" average to compare. Again, those of you above the curve will be in line for annual raises; the rest will not.

I want to put my reasoning and thought process in writing so that I don't hear any more feedback about this—ever. This is the final word on the subject.

I learned this method in graduate school for my MBA at Wharton, which we all know is the most elite business school in the US (and probably worldwide). The behaviors I value in performance are listed in the ranking. These are the only things that make sense and make us profitable. If we aren't profitable, no one gets raises, so it doesn't matter anyway.

You'll notice I added the seventh item just because you all would not stop talking about culture, so there you have it. I have no idea how you are going to evaluate this, and frankly, I don't care as it was never listed in my MBA training at Wharton. So, if you want to drop it altogether, feel free to do so.

I want a competitive culture here, and not everyone is entitled to annual raises—those are entitlements and I refuse to ever start that here. We are a performance-based company, and therefore, only performance above the norm gets rewarded, none below. I gave you all the opportunity to grade your employees and only give raises to A's and B's, but you whined so much about the C's that I took that option off the table. Raises are for winners; losers get nothing. We are not giving out trophies just for showing up. That's not how business works, and these people need to get used to the real world. And I don't care if they cry and go work somewhere else—good riddance to them. Let them be someone else's whiner.

I also do not want to hear any more talk about some of our underperforming teams and that if we rank this way, we are still rewarding the highest of the underperformers. We have to start with something, and if they see that half of their team is getting raises and they are not, maybe they'll work harder so they can be in that top half of the curve.

Conversely, I also don't want to hear any more talk from some of you who have over-performing teams and therefore this isn't fair because half of your team won't get a raise, even though you rank them 9s or 10s. You have to have some way to get them to want to be a 10, so don't reward them for being a 9.

I do realize that no method is completely fair, but this is the one I learned at Wharton; and if it's good enough for the most elite school in the country, it's good enough for all of you.

I'll look forward to seeing your ranking—good luck on getting a raise!

What I say goes,

CEO

LET'S GET REAL

Stack ranking employees was all the rage for a lot of large companies and is still used widely today. It comes in different shapes and sizes, but ultimately, it is not universally regarded as the best way to reward employees. In fact, because it is usually done in complete secrecy, it often has a very negative effect on morale.

First, you want to make sure that all of your employees are paid fairly for the jobs they do. This means there is a range of pay for each position, they know what's required to move from the low end to the high, and there is visibility about the process. It can't be done in secret, and, worse yet, it can't depend on completely subjective factors, such as how much the manager likes someone. That will ultimately get you into legal trouble.

Your ability to get a raise should not be dependent upon how a teammate performs. Employees will not perform well if they are graded on factors outside of their control, including other team members' performance. They either are or are not doing the job well.

In contrast to what our wrong-headed Wharton CEO claims, knowing they will not get a raise, even though they are performing at their peak, will not inspire anyone and will cause them to leave or, worse, become a cultural terrorist inside the organization. If they are a chronic underperformer on an underperforming team and get a raise, what is their inspiration to do better?

Pay needs to be fair. Performance needs to be evaluated fairly. Employees are much happier and perform better when both of these are carefully considered and implemented.

CHAPTER 13

SKANK RANKED

Sent: September 17, 8:00 a.m.
From: Curt, Founder & CEO
To: Tom, Director of HR
Subject: Annual Stack Rank

Tom,

I heard the management team went through the first phase of stack ranking last week. I would have liked to participate, but I am sure the team did a great job. I want to make sure you get Stephanie M. in the top 10 percent of the stack rank. She's amazing. She's on the product development team, right? She's got a great presence in the office and always seems to be on top of her game—a real star in the making. She seems enormously popular with the rest of the staff too.

I heard that she was heading up a couple of social groups in the office as well—that's the team spirit! Make sure she gets a 20 percent pay raise, and I'll make sure I reach out to her and schedule a time for a 1:1 lunch to show my appreciation for her contributions.

I've also got my eye on Jody. Where did you snag her? She sure knows how to work a room. "Large and in charge," if you get my drift. Let's make sure we don't lose her to the competition; I like her style. Put her in the top 20 percent, and give her a 10 percent raise. She's new, so let's keep her hungry and wanting more—I know I do.

Curt

Take a lesson from Curt, Founder and CEO of "Oh, look at that woman over there":

> A most favored event by those at the very tippy-top who want to assert their power over the people and see their shining stars get the recognition they don't deserve is stack ranking, which is a method by which a leadership team takes an entire staff and puts them in order according to their "value" to the company. Once in order, you take some random percentage at the top, middle, and bottom and award pay raises and bonuses for that group. It's as flexible as you want it to be, and easy to defend, because it's entirely subjective and not based on any kind of pesky performance data.

> The most important thing about stack ranking is that it remains on complete secrecy lock-down. No one other than the leadership team can ever see the results of the stack ranking, nor can they ever find out about the hilarity that ensues when you go through the process as you gossip about each and every employee in the company. You should find a trustworthy admin to take notes during your stack-ranking session, and make sure she is ranked near the top so that she's not tempted to leak the results.

> Stack ranking is a great way to penalize employees or "manage them out" for things that are totally unjustifiable otherwise, such as being overweight, ugly, or too shy, or having once cooked fish in the microwave. But make no mistake, no matter how good a job you do to hide the results of your stack-ranking process, your employees all know that you stack rank—so you can count on some

pretty interesting behavior from people who are hell bent on what-
ever-ing their way to the top of the list!

From: Tom, Director of HR
To: Jaime, Director of Product Development
Subject: Annual Stack Rank

Jaime,

Did you approve this pay raise and stack-rank positioning for Steph-anie? If not, I thought you should know that Curt has mandated that she receive a 20 percent pay raise next year. Good luck managing her performance.

As a reminder, she's been with the company for three weeks and her probation period doesn't end until August. Curt knows this, but he wants this raise to happen anyway for some reason.

Tom

In case it isn't abundantly clear in other chapters, we think **stack ranking is one of the worst employee-management practices ever invented and should be avoided at all costs.** It is worthwhile, in fact, to ask if a company you are considering joining does stack ranking as a regular practice, and if so, include it in your decision criteria for accepting a new leadership position.

Stack ranking is nothing more than a popularity contest, especially when done by an ownership/leadership team that is largely disconnected from the mainstream workforce. It gives rise to the loudest and most notable employees and overlooks the quiet contributor. It is a methodology that creates a breeding ground for discrimination, sexism, and favoritism, and it is an open invitation for legal action.

What's worse is that stack ranking, like grading on a curve (discussed in the previous section), assumes that you can only have a subset of top performers. It assumes that in any organization there is a top, middle, and lower level of performance. If you wouldn't assemble a sports team or a military troop based on this kind of thinking, then don't hire or manage with it in your company!

Simply put: nothing good comes from stack ranking. It's demoralizing for your employees, it causes unhealthy competition based on favoritism, and it's bad for developing leaders. Leaders and managers must be taught to evaluate performance on an individual basis as aligned to job requirements, then at the team or group level as aligned to team requirements, then— more holistically—as aligned to company strategy. Peer-to-peer stack ranking takes none of these things into consideration.

But, as in our story above, the real damage is done by the combination of the stack-ranking process and the person at the top who uses it to create their harem of sycophants and/or personal favorites. That leader is subverting the authority and protocol of the organizational chart by making staff management decisions above or around direct managers. If you have a senior leader who is resisting giving up stack ranking, take a good look around them and see if they've created a "court" of favored individuals.

In short: banish stack ranking forever and consider banishing anyone who sings its praises.

CHAPTER 14

BLURRY VISION

Sent: September 17, 8:00 a.m.
From: Chuck, Sales Team Manager
To: Tom, VP of Sales
Subject: Account Assignment

Tom,

Hey man, we need to talk. I've been asked by the team to call a meeting with you to discuss how you've been assigning accounts across the sales team. People were pretty pissed. I guess most of the team has decided just to distribute their accounts how they want, and so they blew off your assignments completely. This really screwed up the CRM system, so they had IT write a script that changed all the assignments. Is that OK, or will that mess up the accounting system and how commissions get calculated? This is a mess, man. Not sure where it went off the rails, but it did.

Chuck

From: Marcia
To: Tom, VP of Sales

Tom,

I got shorted $1,200 on my commission check. Not cool.

Marcia

From: Scott, Accounting Manager
To: Tom, VP of Sales

Tom,

Somehow, we overpaid one of your sales associates by $1,200. How did this happen? Who is in charge of keeping track of whose accounts are assigned to whom? This is a complete mess on the back end.

Scott

From: Buyer, XYZ Company
To: Tom, VP of Sales

Tom,

I've really enjoyed working with your company in the past. And I particularly enjoyed working with Marcia. But she let me know today that she's been taken off of our account by her manager. We've been a great customer and spent a lot of money with your firm—why the change? She didn't seem very happy about it.

Buyer

Take a lesson from Tom, VP of sales and leader in chaos:

> *All for one, and one for all! It's a super-democracy, and a self-governing team with no clear boundaries or rules can result in the top performers rising to the top. So, by all means, let them run the show. Sales people are too squirrelly to manage anyway, so it makes your life easier, right?*

When you leave your team to their own devices, they will certainly self-organize. A lack of clear job descriptions will mean that they simply create their own and do what makes them happy, and who doesn't love that? A happy team means fewer negative GlassDoor reviews for you! In other good news for you, a self-organizing, un-managed team will develop their own company vision and mission, and who knows!? It might even be better than yours.

And, in the spirit of innovation, a lack of clarity about job roles and the definitions of duties will allow you to pit one against another, force people to compete for the same task or job, and disrupt work-flow. When individuals don't meet their goals because of others rather than themselves, chaos ensues. It becomes a dog-eat-dog environment, and the top performers go for the land grab. This is especially successful in managing a sales organization—the more chaos the better!

LET'S GET REAL

Sounds a little like *Lord of the Flies*, doesn't it? There is a reason that organizational design and management hierarchy have remained generally the same as long as they have. There is a reason modern experiments like "holocracies" don't work or don't last. Human beings need leadership, organization, and direction. In any organization, large or small, intentional orga-nizational design with clear job descriptions, roles, and duties is key to peace and success.

According to Gallup, employees need four things to be satisfied: trust, compassion, stability, and hope. Without these, employees are unsure of their boundaries and will neither feel safe nor perform well. Stability says you will have guardrails in place to keep them in the right lane.

When going into battle, each soldier has a clear mission, set of duties, toolkit, and role that they play in the larger theater of war. If a group self-manages to the point of changing their roles or their toolkit, chaos ensues and goals are not met. Such is the result of a work group that goes largely unmanaged or is expected to self-manage.

As a leader, it is your responsibility to make sure the job descriptions for each of your team members are clear, concise, and well communicated to everyone. It is as important for employees to know their peers' job descriptions and expectations as it is for them to know their own. You've had your employees study their own job descriptions, but have you required them to study and understand the JDs of others on their team? Only by doing so can you expect them all to fully understand how they fit together and form a highly functioning team. Innovation and initiative are great, but solid lines make these better, not worse.

CHAPTER 15

TALKING ABOUT FIGHT CLUB

MANAGEMENT TEAM QUARTERLY MEETING AGENDA:

- Warehouse workflow
- Holiday schedules and hours for next week
- Annual performance review deadlines
- ERP system maintenance
- Monthly sales results

CEO: Thanks for coming to the meeting today, guys. We have a lot to cover, so let's get rolling. We've got Sue joining us today—she's a management consultant who is helping me work through some strategic issues. Welcome, Sue. Steve, why don't you get started and give us an update on any changes you have to the warehouse workflow.

Steve: Yep. OK, well, it's looking like we are going to be able to handle the increase in capacity that's forecasted for next week.

Mike will step in and cover Peter's fulfillment duties until we can backfill that position. I've also got some new packing materials to experiment with, but I will probably wait until after the holidays to do that.

Accounting Manager: Is Peter on vacation?

CEO: Let's move on. How about holiday schedules? Who is going to be out between Christmas and New Year's?

Marketing Manager: What happened to Peter?

CEO: I'll pass around the calendar; if you guys can jot down the dates you'll be out, I'll have Stephanie put them in the group calendar.

Consultant: Excuse me? What's going on here? Who is Peter? Where is Peter? And why are we both talking and not talking about Peter?

CEO (voice in head): *Oh my God, I have to stop this conversation right now. They don't need to know that I fired Peter. It's none of their business. If Peter finds out I told people that I fired him, he's going to sue us. Everyone will think I'm an asshole. Peter was a nice guy . . . No one can know. How can I explain my way out of this? He quit? He disappeared? This is a nightmare . . .*

LET'S GET REAL

Imagine being on a senior management team and having the fact that an employee had been terminated purposely withheld from you. Can you think of any logical or rational reason why a manager would do that? Neither could we. Now imagine being an employee—at any level—coming in to your job one day and finding the person who had been sitting at the desk or station next to you for a couple of years suddenly gone. And nobody is talking about it.

There's been no announcement of his or her departure, there is no reason for his or her absence—it's as if the person got raptured! Just up and disappeared. Can you think of any reason on Earth why it would make sense to sow this kind of mystery and mistrust around an employee's departure? Neither could we. But this is a true story, and it happens more often than you'd think.

The first rule of management is to talk about management. That means talking about employee performance and disciplinary measures, and being honest and transparent with your leadership team and staff about departures and other not-so-pleasant news. *Transparency* is the buzzword of the decade, and it's easily misunderstood or misinterpreted. So let's clear up a few things (pun intended):

Transparency works because it builds TRUST, and trust only works when it's based on the TRUTH.

We parted ways with John today as we did not feel that he was the best fit for the position.

John's last day with us was Monday. We wish him all the best in finding a new role that better suits his skill set.

John's last day was today, and we'll be looking to fill the position within the next two weeks. Please join us in wishing him all the best in the future.

These are all perfectly acceptable and respectful ways of saying, "We had to fire John." But saying nothing at all, or fabricating some story, because you fear telling your organization that he was terminated is a huge mistake. Saying nothing is flat-out lying and creates unfair mystery and intrigue. Covering up the termination also doesn't allow you to send a message to your organization that says, "YES, if you don't do your job and perform to our standards, you will lose your job. That's how jobs work!"

Remember, as leaders we are the adults in the room. If you can't adhere to the basic tenets of a healthy and high-functioning management team, then you need to take a close look at your leadership style and the makeup of your leadership team. We believe that there are at least eight core things that should be discussed regularly and with total transparency among a leadership team:

1. Leadership and championship of the mission, vision, values, and purpose:
    Are you all in alignment with these? From your vantage point, can you see anything happening within the company that isn't? Discuss and hold each other accountable.

2. Respect for the organizational chart.

3. Following the RACI (Responsible, Accountable, Consulted, Informed) structure:
    Is everyone in alignment with how the organizational chart works and what the protocols and authorities are? Does everyone understand their roles and the roles of others on the RACI chart? Both of these documents, along with job descriptions at the individual level, should be reviewed and discussed regularly.

4. Complete and immediate transparency:
    Are there any sensitive issues that we need to discuss privately before communicating to the staff? What is our strategy for communicating sensitive issues to the staff? Are we being transparent with each other and holding each other accountable for transparency among our staff?

5. Unity and consensus in decision making:
    Have we communicated and debated critical deci-
    sion-making among the management team prior to
    the decision being made? Do we have consensus on
    strategy? We may differ on tactics, but must have con-
    sensus on strategy and confirm regularly that we do.

6. Discipline and time commitment:
    Are we, as a team, committed to each other, and have
    we made time for actually managing as a team?

7. Triads and the buddy system:
    Does anyone feel like they are on an island? If so,
    why? And what will we do about it?

8. Financial visibility:
    Lastly, does everyone on the leadership team know
    how we are doing financially? Do they know what role
    they and their team play in building value and prof-
    itability for the organization? (We'll talk more about
    this last point in our next book, *How (NOT) to Create a
    Winning Strategy.*)

The first rule of a good management team is to talk about
management with your team. Seems like a no-brainer, but you'd
be surprised at how many teams talk about everything except
management. Have the conversation with your team, and use
the above checklist to make sure you're transparent and aligned

CHAPTER 16

LOYALTY IS THE NEW COCAINE

FROM THE NARCISSIST'S GUIDE TO SELECTING TEAM MEMBERS

As we see from our current political leadership, loyalty is the number one criterion to ascertain whether someone is worthy of being on our team. Why wouldn't it be?? If you don't have loyalty from your team, you are not a leader—period.

I recommend getting loyalty pledges from all of the people that work for you. Some will balk, so it's quite simple to let them know their job is one the line if they refuse to participate. Now, unlike a non-compete or non-disclosure agreement, you don't have to pay anything for this. Essentially, their paycheck is all you have to commit to! Think of the beauty in that! I seriously don't understand why more companies don't take advantage of this rarely used, incredibly successful tactic.

Let's think about it in practical terms. You expect loyalty—but yet, you can't be sure that your people are. And what makes an incredibly strong team? *Loyalty.* Bingo! Use the loyalty pledge. You can consider getting it verbally, which may be sufficient in some cases, but in most cases I would recommend getting it in writing. The problem with verbal is that the bastards will turn coat on you, and then you have to call them liars and hope that your word is stronger than theirs. If you're in the position of power and authority, your word over their word is usually enough. However, having a loyalty pledge in writing is always the ace in the hole when they start dishing on you to the failing New York Times.

Getting this agreement in writing is nothing short of brilliance in leadership terms. It feels great—like a shot of the best drug in the world straight into the arm—at least in the moment. It feels even better when you get the chance to enforce it as soon as one of the little rats jumps ship and reveals less than flattering details about you. But getting it in writing can be tricky. First, your HR department will tell you that although it's not strictly illegal, it's highly unethical. Well, we all know that ethics are a matter of interpretation, so forget about those. They are what *you* say they are. And if *you* say them louder and longer than someone else, *you* win. Believe me, it works.

Once you are past the pain-in-the-ass HR and legal types, you simply craft a letter that says *this is my loyalty pledge to you, and whatever you do or say, I will support and abide by and never, ever reveal any doubts, questions, or otherwise countervailing points of view.*

The conversation with your team can be tricky so I recommend the approach of meeting with all of them as a team and laying it out for them. Explain that as a leader, it's fundamental to the success of the team that your authority, prowess, and decision-making ability never be questioned. When they look at you with that stupid, questioning, or quizzical look, you face them off and say, "Do you have a problem with this pledge?" And then, "Are you the first who will show me disrespect and disloyalty?" I always like throwing in the disrespect aspect of it because if they're stupid enough to have a conscience, this term will cut to the bone. Of course, they will back down and it'll just be a great lesson to the rest of the team. The leader is all powerful and that they are not—which is exactly how you want it. If you get some smart ass who is all indignant because you are requiring this pledge, fire him or her on the spot and remind them that you will sue their ass off if they violate the confidentiality agreement. Boom! You just showed everyone who's in charge.

Usually, you'll get full compliance at that point. But you may detect a few outliers that have gotten together to question your competence. It's vitally important to cut these weeds down as quick as you see them. Invite them into your office for a friendly chat and remind them that they are special to you. Butter them up with whatever you know will make them feel good, and then ask why they haven't signed their agreement. Tell them that they are the chosen one, the heir apparent—they'll never talk to their peers to find out you said the same thing to the rest of them. You know they're stupid; otherwise they would be in your job, right? So, don't start to give them credit now for being smarter than they are.

Once you are relatively sure you have everyone on board with pledging loyalty and fealty to you and only you, now for the coup de gras. Get everyone together and have them say nice things about you, particularly about your stellar leadership skills so the rest of the group can hear. Something like, "I am so grateful that Don selected me to be on his team. I can't wait to learn more from him about leadership and am happy to pledge my loyalty." A few specifics are great but more importantly, you want the pledges.

Once you have these from your team and rid yourself of the traitors, you're the golden boy. Of course, this type of loyalty can always backfire if you're not careful about constantly weeding out for the miscreants and the two-timers. Sometimes just firing someone because you're suspicious—without any proof—will do the trick. Stay on it and you'll have a team of sycophants second to none!

LET'S GET REAL

Loyalty is good to have but true loyalty is earned. Having loyalty pledges in writing or verbally is counterproductive to what you are trying to achieve. If loyalty is required, it's not loyalty—it's servitude and that will only go so far. Forced loyalty will almost always backfire on you because people don't like to be forced into anything.

If you have earned the loyalty of your team—which is helpful for effective leadership—they will know it's optional. You need to show them every day why they have made a good choice to support you as leader. Not because their job depends on it, but because they believe in your leadership. Forced loyalty is fake loyalty. It will never last and is almost worse than having none at all because now you've created moles and enemies.

Be an authentic leader, own your mistakes and successes, recognize the contributions of others, and help them grow into leaders. These principles will gain you the highest level of loyalty: Respect.

SECTION 3

GIFTING GREATNESS

You will never see "She made me what I am today" written on anyone's tombstone. But a leader's job is just that: identifying the individual strengths that each team member comes to the table with; coaxing, leading, training, cajoling, and developing those strengths into greatness. As a leader, you will come with specific skills and deficits; knowing both will help you help others achieve their potential.

Insecure leaders worry that a team member will overshadow them and take credit—or worse, take their job. Confident leaders give credit and are thrilled when one of their team surpasses them. It's considered a job well done. Unfortunately, that is becoming a rarity in our culture. Leaders who fear loss of stature, importance, or position will never let others overshadow them, yet a real leader's job is to let all those who work for them shine as bright as they possibly can.

Everyone has gifts; some just never get a chance to open them. As a leader, making sure there is no gift left unopened is your job. Like watching a kid open the gift they asked Santa for, as a leader you will and *should* have that same excitement when someone on your team succeeds. It's perfectly OK to have that moment of doubt, that quick little pang of *wow, that used to be me,* but if it's more than a moment of angst, you've just stepped in it. It's about them, not you.

Parents try as hard as they can to pave the road for their children and make it as easy as possible to succeed. Unfortunately, as well intended as this may be, it does not always work out. If the child never learns how to solve a problem, they will lash out when faced with one and wait for someone else to fix it rather than try to fix it themselves. Leaders often try to make it easy for their teams to succeed, fixing mistakes or telling them what path to take. Individuals will only find their own leadership style and gifts by doing it themselves—mistakes and all. The leader's job is to make sure none of the mistakes are fatal. Skinned knees and broken bones may happen, and from these people will learn how to self-correct. Patience is a requirement of the leader when developing people, as is having the fortitude to NOT cover the kids in bubble wrap to keep them from getting hurt.

Gifting greatness is not only recognizing the unique contributions of everyone on the team, but also being a model of what good leadership looks like. Words and actions must be consistent and authentic—do what you say you will do, model what you want in your team. Everyone smells BS. No matter the deodorizer you choose to cover it, BS still stinks.

When a leader makes a mistake, it needs to be acknowledged, not covered up. "There is learning in them there hills," as they say—no screwup is made without a chance to learn, and a good leader shows the way by owning it. Give your team a model they can start with and make their own. Only then will their greatness, not yours, find a voice.

CHAPTER 17

SHOW ME THE MONEY

From: Amy Hoohoo, Director of HR
To: Jeff Parson
Subject: Job Offer

Dear Jeff,

We are pleased to present you with this formal offer for employment with the Acme Corporation as our new director of corporate communications. This is a full-time salaried position located in Atlanta, Georgia, that reports to our senior vice president of marketing, Jill Smith.

The starting salary for this position will be $120,000 per year. Please see attached for your eligibility and details of both our 401(k) program and our employee benefits.

It is a position that includes a fair amount of business travel, as we have discussed. Please review the attached travel policy and let me know if you have any questions.

Sincerely,

Amy Hoohoo
Director of Human Resources

One year later…

Sent: September 1, 9:00 a.m.
From: Jill Smith, SVP of Marketing
To: Amy Hoohoo, Director of HR
Subject: Jeff's Salary

Amy,

In preparation for this year's performance and salary reviews, I received the following table of salary histories for my staff. This says that Jeff's salary is $220,000. Must be a mistake—I hired him at $120K. Can you make sure this is corrected and sent back to me?

Thanks,

Jill

Sent: September 1, 11:30 a.m.
From: Amy Hoohoo, Director of HR
To: Jill Smith, SVP of Marketing
Subject: RE: Jeff's Salary

Jill,

No mistake there. That's what Jeff's salary has been since day one. Did Curt not tell you that he had me change the offer letter before I sent it to Jeff last year? He was really worried we wouldn't get him for $120K, so he bumped it up a little.

Amy

Sent: September 1, 11:55 a.m.
From: Curt Collins, Sales Director
To: Jill Smith, SVP of Marketing
Subject: Jeff's Salary

Jill,

I didn't trust you to be able to hire him at that low salary. And I knew you wouldn't listen to me, so I intercepted the offer letter, increased the amount, and had Amy send it. I figured I'd get around to telling you or that you'd see a payroll report before now, but that doesn't seem to have happened. I can understand why you're upset, especially given that you and Jeff aren't getting along that well.

Curt

Sent: September 1, 11:59 a.m.
From: Jill Smith, SVP of Marketing
To: Curt Collins, Sales Director
Subject: RE: Jeff's Salary

Curt,

My direct-report employee makes $80K more than I do? Seriously? And you think he's not performing because we're not getting along well? How about his pay is completely out of line with his job description and he has no idea where he actually sits in the order of things around here?

Thanks a lot!

Jill

LET'S GET REAL

Anyone who has ever been in middle management knows what it feels like to be tasked with hiring top talent but not given enough budget to do so. But there are also scenarios where employees are paid too much or bonused too much. Either way, not having the right compensation package at the individual level and the right—and consistent!—compensation philosophy at the corporate level can wreak absolute havoc on an organization. Let's take a look at how either of these can happen and how we can prevent it.

PAYING TOO MUCH

Jill's story about an executive at her company literally hijacking an offer letter that was under her authority is a true but extreme anecdote about how you can start off on the wrong foot with a compensation package, but the result is not uncommon at all. Oftentimes, we convince ourselves that we've found a unicorn, the perfect fit for the job, the ideal candidate, and we fall head over heels.

We are so afraid we're going to lose him or her to the competition, we front-load the compensation package with everything we've got. And we literally buy him or her off the market. Of course, we have to do all kinds of fancy footwork to rationalize it in our budget—but we convince ourselves it's worth it. We make the offer, and WE WIN. We got 'em.

But here's the rub: Does that compensation package allow you to manage your new hire for continuous growth and improvement? That's different than just getting the hire made, and often we forget that, as hiring managers, it's not just our job to hire top talent, it's to manage that talent to add real growth and value to the company over time. Mark our words: you cannot do that if you overpay someone from the get-go. Not only because it doesn't give you the room to increase the pay incrementally over time, but because it creates a scenario in which that employee compares their pay with pay outside of the company, causing them to misalign their job description with their pay.

Logic might say that if you pay someone well, they will do a great job; however, if you pay them over the pay scale of the job you've hired them to do, they won't do the job at all. Make sense? Well, in Jill's true story, Jeff was impossible to manage because he thought he was above the tasks she asked him to complete—and he was right! With a $100K differential on what the job was worth and what he was being paid to do the job, it made perfect sense that he wasn't performing.

And that wasn't fair to anyone involved.

PAYING TOO LITTLE

There is nothing to be happy about if you just landed a new hire for significantly less than you thought you were going to have to pay or less than market value. If you are getting away with paying less than market value, it's probably because your candidate didn't know their value or simply did a poor job of negotiating. There should be no pride in taking advantage of someone by paying them less than what they are worth for a job simply because you can get away with it.

There are going to be performance problems associated with underpaying employees. They will eventually learn that they are not being paid what they are worth, they will be resentful, they will underperform, and, ultimately, they will leave. It seems like a no-brainer when it comes to under- or overpaying, but it's probably more the norm than the exception in business today.

PAYING JUUUUUST RIIIIGHT

There are three important words to remember to get it just right: **fair market value**. If the most important tenet of your compensation policy is fair market value, you really can't go wrong. What it means is that you will have to make an effort—or pay a professional to do the research for you—to always know where the fair market values in your industry stand. The goal is to know the values so well that you can build a pay scale that you can stick to and be proud of. If you commit to fair market value and never allow exceptions, you'll land in the *juuuuust riiiiight* range every time.

If you want to ensure you are always in the safe zone, consider hiring an HR professional or compensation specialist to do the following:

- Create a documented compensation philosophy and require all staff members to read it.

- Create packages that are simple but flexible. Never create a package that is difficult to understand or calculate, or impossible to achieve.

- Create compensation ranges for every role or set of roles in your company and never, ever deviate from them. If there are exceptions, they aren't rules.

- Use the same structure and logic in every department. Differing structures simply invites misunderstanding about fairness.

- Prepare to pay fair market value for every role in your company.

- Assume your payroll report will accidentally be forwarded to everyone in the company someday, and be ready to stand by every decision ever made related to pay.

CHAPTER 18

TITLES ARE FOREVER

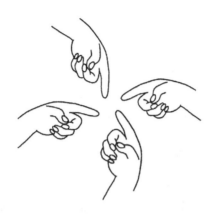

Sent: September 20
From: CEO
To: HR
Subject: Chief of Compassion

Jennifer,

Please prepare a promotion package for Randy. I believe this new role, Chief of Compassion, will be much better suited to what he does on a regular basis. We need someone with his empathy and ability to connect with our customers and employees.

I know you and I have discussed that some of what he does actually fits into the HR department, but I don't see it that way. I know you want the title of Chief of Staff, and at some point, we may revisit it.

For now, let's just do this one. Give him only about a 5 percent bump in pay because it's not a real C-level job, but it looks good and he deserves it. He will be included in the C-suite meetings, but only so he can help us be a bit more compassionate. He won't have any direct reports or any real authority, so make sure to outline that in his letter. I don't want him getting any ideas.

Also, let's move Jane and Jim Bob up to VP levels. I know they'll be passing up the director level altogether, but they've achieved such great results this past year. I think they deserve the bump. They can keep their same teams—just have it be a direct line to their managers, the other VPs, again, not a real change in authority, just a bump for a recognition of a job well done.

Let me know if you have any questions.

LeRoy

Sent: September 20
From: HR
To: CEO
Subject: Chief of Compassion

LeRoy,

I'm a little confused by this title. I could find no comparable title anywhere, so can't find any comps for pay. Also, I'm not sure how to even write a job description for it, let alone map out how he can be successful at it. I'm worried that we are setting a dangerous precedent for unreal job titles. Can you please give me more detail on how this person will succeed and what they should be doing?

Regarding the bump for Jane and Jim Bob: Have you spoken to their managers about this? Both of the managers have expressed grave doubts that these two should move up to director, let alone VP, level. Can we discuss this before you move ahead with it? Again, I'm worried that we are setting a dangerous precedent regarding promotions that could lead to a free-for-all and more of a popularity contest.

The last issue is that we still have Steve to consider. You bumped him to director last year, and he has completely failed. As a sales guy he was great, but he can't manage his way out of a paper bag. Everyone thinks we should move him back to sales, but they don't want me to take away his title. If he's one of the sales people, he can't have the director title. And we'll have to move his pay back in line with the rest of the outside sales team.

How would you like me to proceed on these?

Jennifer

Sent: September 21
From: CEO
To: HR
Subject: Chief of Compassion and Other Matters

Jennifer,

As we discussed multiple times, this is a brand-new innovative position, so I'm certain you won't find comps—we are the first! Don't worry about a job description; we'll just play it by ear. If I'm happy with his performance at the end of the year, he'll get to keep the title. If not, we'll just move him back to his old role.

Jim Bob and Jane came from my old company, with much higher titles than we started them at, so these promotions have been a long time coming. I know them better than their managers, and I am completely comfortable moving them into these roles. I am fairly confident they will grow into them in due time. Their managers are just jealous because I have a closer relationship with Jim Bob and Jane due to our previous work relationship—and that I am the godfather to Jane's kids. Besides, I already informed them about it. Your role is merely to make it formal. No need to discuss it further.

Just move Steve back to sales and take away the title. I'm tired of everyone whining about this one. He sucked as sales director, and if he wants to keep his job, he can go back to his old role. He can go talk with Randy as our new Chief of Compassion if he wants a shoulder to cry on. I'm done with it.

LeRoy

LET'S GET REAL

These days it's trendy to have new and trendy titles: Director of First Impressions, Chief Inspiration Officer, Chief Evangelist, Chief Risk Officer, Chief Fun Officer, and Chief Diversity Officer. C-suite titles should be for those major functions that are needed to run the company, executives, operations, sales and marketing, finance, and technology or IT. Occasionally you'll have research and development in that mix, but only if that is a significant product or service area for the company.

The problem with made-up titles is that they come with real salaries, job descriptions, and expectations. Someone has to put that on their résumé and explain to someone else what they did in that position. Ill-defined positions reflect poorly on both the employees and the company. It can get muddy very quickly. Decide on the business structure for the organization, and stick to it with defined paths for employees to move through the ranks if they choose to. Make sure that what is expected and required to succeed is crystal clear. Pay fairly based on comparable positions at like-sized organizations in similar regions.

When we promote someone based on anything other than real reasons—such as actually earning it—there are all sorts of problems that follow: entitlement, fiefdoms, pay inflation, incompetence, unclear expectations, and resentment. When we finally decide that this person is failing, it's usually too late to save them. No one wants to move back to their old role and old pay. It's humiliating.

Moving people up to garner loyalty is also a bad reason to promote and title creep. It wreaks havoc on the team and shreds the leader's role as an impartial arbiter of talent and judgement. Titles need to be meaningful, employees need to know how to succeed, pay needs to follow titles, and all of it needs to be transparent.

CHAPTER 19

LESSONS LEARNED ARE 4 LOSERS

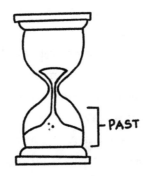

NOTES FOR MY LEADERSHIP MEMOIR:

Let's take a lesson from Tom, the newly minted and inexperienced CEO. When you're the new CEO on the block, everyone is looking at you to do great things. Some, like your employees and especially the leadership team, are a little wary and waiting to see whether you prove yourself or fail. They hold off a bit on hitching their wagon to yours—watching out for their own butts. The board brought you on to shake things up, so you're on a short time frame to prove yourself. Generally speaking, you're also given a lot of leeway to do whatever you want.

I took over a great organization that was a cash cow after a buyout, and the board wanted me to grow it in three years and triple the multiple. With that kind of cash being thrown off, how could I lose? The old CEO offered to spend time with me and walk me through some of the more nuanced areas of the company, but why waste the time? I didn't plan to do anything he had done, so I didn't want to be cluttered up with what didn't work. I love how our US presidents leave letters for their successors with what are supposed to be inspirational and helpful lessons learned—does anyone really read those? If you're the one in the Oval Office now, why would you even care? You have new ground to plow and great things to accomplish. They were part of yesterday, not tomorrow. (Note to self: Remember that phrase for my memoir)

The business was not complicated. First order of business was to get rid of the senior team and bring in my own. Not a big deal that it was two totally unrelated types of business—they'll learn quickly, they always have. Business is business. Once they're in place, they can tell me how they think we should proceed. I only kept the CFO and got rid of the overpaid, undereducated bunch of freeloaders anyway, so no loss with them.

My team went right to work, except for the COO, who had to take some personal time off between gigs, which cost us about three months. Not a problem, though, as I spent the time introducing myself to the customers and independent contractors that delivered our services. And might as well take advantage of the great city while I was here! A little R&R on the company dime is just what the doctor ordered.

OK, back to business. My team recommended we roll out three new and radical programs to jump-start growth. I love it. They were new and different and would really shake things up. We rolled them out with great fanfare (the secret is always in the marketing pitch behind any new initiative), and they were widely received as new and innovative—mostly by the staff, which I found to be very supportive. I had heard a few rumors that this had been tried before, but my comeback was, "Not like I am doing it!" The real pushback came from the field contractors. They started raising alarm bells and telling me I didn't know what I was doing. First, I was shocked that these assholes were telling me what to do with such disrespect. Then I realized they were really just frustrated wannabe CEOs who failed and were now contractors. What did I care what they thought?

A year into our innovations, I started to hear a daily drumbeat of messages of "we've tried this before and it failed," "we're not getting support from the field," "this is like Groundhog Day," and "it's déjà vu all over again." We were not getting the results, and in fact we had moved backward. The bottom line was shrinking before my eyes. Why didn't they tell me all this before? The board was not happy.

I brought the leadership team together and asked them to give me a rundown of what wasn't working. Well, the floodgates opened up and they dumped all over me that I didn't listen to what had already been done and was ignoring the fact that all of these initiatives were not new, just retreads. I exploded at the team. How could they have let me down like this? I had asked them to vet these ideas, so of course I thought they were new. How could I possibly have known that they had been tried before, when my team let me down so badly?

Of course, I was going to have to make a lesson of these guys. One of them would have to go. I would have to make one of them a scapegoat. Unfortunately, I decided to let the COO go since she took three months to actually get here—she's the one who missed the due diligence. It's not my job to look backward; it was hers, and she should have presented only new and fresh ideas.

When faced with a bad plan, or a plan that has been tried before, resist the urge to go back and look at lessons learned. Remember, success only comes through trying out new things and moving as fast as possible away from failures until you hit on one that works. (Another gem for my leadership book.)

LET'S GET REAL

Ignoring the wealth of knowledge from our predecessors or outgoing leadership is a reckless—sometimes fatal—mistake. Sometimes it can be due to pure hubris, such as in our current political leadership. Sometimes it can be due to ignorance or even fear. Fear of failure or of doing anything the same way as it was done in the past is not an excuse to overlook the lessons of others. But both past successes and failures have invaluable lessons for every leader.

When developing leaders, you want to share examples with them of what has worked for you and what has not. Ignoring those, you're casting them out to sea without a safety rope. They might make it...but they might not. Why take that chance?

One of the great benefits of using the past as context for your decisions going forward is that you will save enormous amounts of time and resources. Why would you try something that failed in the past in exactly the same way? Learn through a debrief what didn't go well, and try something different. Time and money are things we never get back, so why would you spend the same amount on a clunker that won't drive? You wouldn't.

Don't waste your precious leadership capital without carefully considering the lessons from the past. (Note to self: Put that in a leadership book! Oh yeah, I am!)

CHAPTER 20

ACCOUNTABILITY-FREE WORKPLACES

Sent: September 9
From: CEO
To: Executive Team
Subject: Launch Date for New Warehouse in Texas

Team,

Per our 2019 strategic plan, we were supposed to have a timeline worked out for the new warehouse in Texas. At our last meeting, we agreed that you all would get together to agree on something and put it in writing so we could review.

Let's set up a meeting for later this week to see where we are.

Thanks.

Sent: September 10
From: Tom T.
To: CEO
Subject: RE: Launch Date for New Warehouse in Texas

Hey Boss Man,

My bad. I meant to set up that meeting but didn't do it because Jane was unavailable on the day we wanted to meet. Sorry, I'll get right on that. Let's hold off on the bigger meeting till we have something to show you. No worries, we're on it!

Tom

Sent: September 10
From: Jane
To: CEO
Subject: RE: Launch Date for New Warehouse in Texas

John,

I meant to bring this to your attention, so my apologies for having forgotten. Tom was going to set up a meeting, but then some of us had conflicts with the date, but he never rescheduled. I'll make sure we get someone on the calendar to discuss.

Jane

Sent: September 24
From: CEO
To: Executive Team

Subject: Launch Date for New Warehouse in Texas

Hey Guys,

I heard from Tom T. and Jane that you all were going to meet to go over the timeline for the new warehouse. Did that ever happen? Remember when we met in January for our strategic planning that we wanted to have it operational by June of 2019. I'm a little worried we will bump up against the date if we don't get moving soon! Thanks in advance for your attention to this matter.

John, CEO

Sent: September 25
From: Tom T.
To: CEO
Subject: RE: Launch Date for New Warehouse in Texas

Sorry, Boss. We got waylaid with the new order from Amazon that came in last week. I'll get right on it!

Tom

Sent: September 26
From: Jane
To: CEO
Subject: RE: Launch Date for New Warehouse in Texas

John,

Tom T. has not set up that meeting that he promised a few weeks ago. Would you like me to set it up for everyone?

Jane

Sent: September 30
From: CEO
To: Jane
Subject: RE: RE: Launch Date for New Warehouse in Texas

Sure. I'd like to meet first of next month about it, so if you guys could get on it, that will work.

John, CEO

Sent: October 21
From: CEO
To: Executive Team
Subject: Launch Date for New Warehouse in Texas

Guys,

Did you ever meet to come up with the timeline? I would like to review so we can get moving because Finance told me we need to make some budget commitments if we're really doing this thing.

Thanks

Sent: October 30
From: Tom T.
To: CEO
Subject: RE: Launch Date for New Warehouse in Texas

Boss, we're on it. Last meeting got canceled because Finance didn't get us the budget numbers, so will get it scheduled ASAP.

Tom

Sent: December 1
From: CEO
To: Exec. Team
Subject: Launch Date for New Warehouse in Texas

Hey guys,

I never heard back from anyone on the plan. Let's plan to address it in our December 15 budget meeting. We'll just add some time to that meeting.

Sent: January 15
From: CEO
To: Executive Team
Subject: Strategic Planning Meeting

Team,

It's that time of year again to plan for our strategic planning session.

Like last year, let's take a day to review what we've accomplished and look at what we need to do going forward. We'll need to decide what we're doing about the new warehouse since we didn't get it into the budget for 2019 and we didn't get to talk about it at our December meeting. Did we ever get that timeline? Just bring it to our strat plan meeting, and we can decide to move forward or push the decision out till the fall.

Thanks,

John, CEO

LET'S GET REAL

In the workplace, "stuff" happens to get in the way of the "stuff" we said we wanted to do. Sometimes it's important stuff; most of the time it's not. Accountability-free workplaces are fun for everyone; no one is really held accountable for anything other than what they want to do each day. Chaos sets in when you have everyone marching to the beat of their own drum—and plans become meaningless.

Accountability starts with leadership. If the CEO can't hold people accountable, why should anyone else? Employees will watch what the leader does and do the same. If it doesn't fit with their values or style, they will leave. Unfortunately for most companies, good employees will not hang out at a place that is devoid of accountability. They don't want to be measured by and against people who aren't accountable. Fundamentally, they want to succeed. If you never know where the goal post is, how can you succeed? You can't—because anything goes.

Our hapless John is not an atypical leader. He asks for things, and he sort of knows what he wants done, but he mimics his employees' bad behavior. So which came first, the chicken or the egg? Lack of leader accountability or follower accountability?

First, he sets no specifics or dates for when he expects something—so why should anyone else? Second, he makes it sound like whatever he is asking for is optional or "whenever they get around to it." Third, he doesn't bother to follow up in a timely manner, so why should they? Lastly, there are absolutely no consequences for NOT delivering on the most basic of requests, a timeline for a new project. There were no consequences for missing the opportunity of the warehouse—if it was even a real opportunity.

When holding people accountable, the three elements to look for are awareness, ability, and commitment. When something doesn't happen, make sure the person or persons are aware of what the expectation is and when you expect to get it. Next, make sure they have the ability to do what it is you are asking of them. Lastly, check that you have commitment from all parties involved.

At the executive leadership level, we can likely expect that they are aware and also have the ability. In John's case, it was likely a lack of commitment by his entire team to get it done. John's inability to hold them accountable potentially cost the organization a strategic move. Ultimately, lack of accountability will cost companies money, people, and jobs.

CHAPTER 21

SILENCE IS NOT GOLDEN

It landed on Carol's desk with the muffled thump of a dead body wrapped in a heavy, wet flannel blanket.

A neat but heavy package, it was a nine-by-twelve-inch envelope no less than four inches thick. FedEx had delivered it that morning, and the receptionist casually swung it by after her lunch break. How could she have known that within this package lay the next six months of utter and complete hell? Hell in a FedEx Overnight envelope.

When she opened it, it didn't hiss. Smoke didn't slowly escape from its hellish guts. It wasn't hot or even warm to the touch. But when she pulled the neatly stacked, stapled, stitched, and clipped papers from the envelope and got the first view of its contents...it STUNG. And stung mightily, and repeatedly.

There they were, the crisp, clean white pages, staring at her, the stinging words—the important words—flying off the page and stinging her directly in the eyeballs:

IN THE MATTER OF...

DEFENDANT

PURSUANT TO...

You are hereby NOTIFIED...

And the numbers...The numbers cascading down the left margin of what would be more than a hundred pages seemed to never end.

1.

1.1

1.2

1.3

1.4 And the pages of text that would follow, as the numbers droned on and on, and the text droned on and on,

1.5 were carefully double-spaced, as if designed to ensure that she was subjected to the maximum

1.6 amount of pain with each and every word, each and every sentence. Drip, drip, drip . . .

The PTSD of her divorce came screaming back and filled her with dread. What was this? What had gone wrong? What did she miss? It had been five years; how could this not have been resolved? Once her head stopped spinning and the blur of the words and numbers and the vibration of the white space on the paper ceased, she was able to take a closer look.

WRONGFUL TERMINATION

Wrongful termination? Of whom? She quickly surmised that with fewer than a hundred employees in her company, surely she would know if someone had been wrongfully terminated. Surely she would know if

there had been an "unpleasant departure," as they say in the business. But nothing came to mind. She read on:

JAMES SMITH

James, Jim, Jimmy, Jimbo? Nope. Who is James Smith? Who the hell is (or was) James Smith, and when did he work here, who did he report to, and why is he suing us for wrongful termination?

She snatched the org chart off of her bulletin board. Inspecting box after box, in every branch office—BOOM!—she finally found a small box in the lower left corner of the PowerPoint-generated org chart: James Smith, receptionist, Los Angeles branch. *We had a receptionist in the LA office?* This was news to her. It was either in the "news" or detailed-information-she-didn't-care-about-until-now category. It would require a call to the LA branch manager to put her finger on it.

He reminded her that James had been hired last summer, so he was with the company just over a year. He missed the company's annual meeting due to an illness, and he missed the company's summer picnic because he was getting married the same weekend. Totally valid excuses. The LA branch manager explained that he'd made the decision to hire a receptionist even though other branches didn't have receptionists because he thought it would look good to visitors. There wasn't much for the person to do in a three-person office, but that was no matter.

So the detailed-information-she-didn't-care-about-until-now opened up a new category of information: activities-that-her-own-management-team-was-engaging-in-and-not-telling-her-about.

And there she sat—totally exposed. Without even reading the rest of the lawsuit, she felt totally blindsided, and the air was knocked clean out of her. She had no idea who this person was, why he had been hired, what he had been hired to do, and why—really—he had been fired. She was at the mercy of a branch manager that had gone rogue, but she didn't know what kind of rogue.

What had gone wrong? And what would happen next?

LET'S GET REAL

Any parent instinctively knows that if you have more than fifteen seconds of silence from toddlers—who aren't sleeping soundly—in another room, you've got big trouble. Fifteen seconds of silence could be a jelly bean up a nose. Thirty seconds of silence could be a permanent-marker masterpiece on the kitchen wall. A full minute of silence could be a full-blown journey into the uppermost shelves of an open refrigerator.

But silence in the workplace can go on much longer than a minute. It can be days, weeks, months, even years. If a leader isn't listening or doesn't have the proper controls in place for communication and accountability from those who should be listening, things can go horribly wrong. By the time they are clued in and everything is brought to light, it's too late.

Carol's company was growing, and she was stepping back from the day-to-day. It was becoming more and more difficult for her to personally know each and every employee. She'd gotten pretty good at dealing with that awkward moment of meeting someone for the first time after they had been working at her company for six months. Carol felt like she had a solid leadership team in place, and she did—right up until she didn't. She liked giving them the space and autonomy to make decisions on their own. She didn't want to be "the meddler."

But her branch manager made a series of fatal errors that ended in a lawsuit, and they all were born out of silence. He made a hire into a new, untested role *and* told no one above him. He hired a qualified person but didn't communicate the nature, goals, or career path of the role. He didn't train or onboard the hire with any kind of structure or rigor. He didn't help assimilate the person into the company. He hired a phone answerer, plunked him down at a desk with a phone, and walked away.

The details of James's termination and the outcome of the lawsuit are best saved for another chapter titled "How Not to Not Settle a Lawsuit," but the moral of the story thus far is: *Great companies and great people can fail in silence.*

All companies are people companies, and people are always a company's greatest assets. When we don't communicate or put in controls and rigor for collaboration and communication, the rails bend and things can head in unintended directions.

CHAPTER 22

TYPE A IS FOR A$$HOLE

Sent: September 17
From: CEO
To: Exec. Team
Subject: Anti-Harassment Training

OK, guys,

It's that time of year again that we have to sit through listening to HR tell us how we're supposed to behave. So show up, behave, and put your time in. I don't expect any of you to fail this little exercise!

Remember, leaders lead and losers don't. Which one are you?!!

Your Boss

FROM THE DESK OF A SICK-OF-THIS-CRAP CEO:

Realistically, I moved up through the ranks the hard way in this organization. No time for this pansy-assed pussyfooting around with everyone's feelings. Men were men, women were women, and if you can take over a room and perform, you move to the top of the food chain. If you're at the bottom, you're where you should be.

No time to give a hand down because you're always reaching for that next wrung up. The only reason to look behind you is to make sure no little f'er is hanging on your coattail trying to get a ride up. Cut that sucker off immediately. They provide absolutely no benefit to you if they're not willing to make it on their own.

I had to schedule this stupid HR thing because of the complaints. Jesus. In my day you just sucked it up. I don't have a problem with anyone's race, ethnicity, gender, or anything else, for that matter, except lack of balls. If you don't have balls, you don't belong in leadership.

Kill or be killed, and NEVER show any sign of weakness. That's why I hate these stupid things, because it's like we're supposed to be soft and cuddly to all these losers who don't know their ass from a hole in the ground.

I did take this up with the board, but got shot down because of that last little complaint against me. They said I was a little "too aggressive" in telling our female sales manager what I thought of her piss-poor performance. What was I supposed to tell her? She FAILED!! We will not be meeting our numbers this quarter, and bonuses are on the line, so it's on her!! Unfortunately, the board had to settle with her when she left after our meeting, and they're holding me accountable for it. Such pushovers.

Leadership is all about taking charge, no matter what. Show weakness and you lose. Period. There is not a one of my Harvard classmates who would have any respect for me if I was passive. Even passive-aggressive is for wussies.

If you want to show leadership, show strength! Be out front with it! Call people out when they don't perform, and you'll be respected. My team respects me. In fact, they probably fear me, which is a good thing. You need to keep people on their toes, never knowing where you stand, so they are always looking for praise or favor. That's strength.

I teach all my leaders to be tough, to take a stand, and to never back down. Even when faced with evidence that would show you were wrong—DON'T BACK DOWN!! They'll come after you like a pack of hyenas if you do. This was how I learned how to be a leader and how I became the successful CEO of a Fortune 500 company. Why should I look in the mirror or change now?

This is how they should teach these damn HR seminars: tough, muddier leadership. Those who don't survive weren't meant to be in the race. Period.

LET'S GET REAL

"Type A" usually refers to go-getters, the people who can handle a lot and those who want to win. These traits are good for a team; however, the in-your-face asshole is not good. No one responds well to working with or working for this type of person. If you have one on your team and can't point out to them the error of their ways, point them to the door.

If you are the leader of the team, it's great to be tough. It's also great to listen and be willing to be wrong. Great leaders look at all sides of the Rubik's Cube to see the best way to put it together, not just their way. When you have an asshole on the team, good players will usually try to play nice with them or even try to get them to come over to the light.

A true asshole, like our CEO above, will crush them like a bug. He will perceive their invitation as a sign of weakness and take a shot at them. Someone who has learned from an example like this might be redeemable. If they can be persuaded to see a different way to get what they want, one that involves teamwork, cooperation, and collaboration, they might work out. If not, they're an asshole and need to be removed from the team—like yesterday.

Building a great team starts with talent and requires looking for a fit that aligns with the company's values. You don't all need to be carbon copies of one another. In fact, it's best if there is diversity. Diversity breeds innovation and equality, which then provides opportunities for all. Assholes love other assholes because it's like looking in the mirror and loving what they see: themselves. Assholes never grow, they just replicate like cockroaches, and then it's time for the exterminator.

Good Type As are driven, hard-working, talented individuals who look out for the team as much as they look out for themselves. Type A assholes are always going to be a bad fit for a team—and usually lead to lawsuits—with time and money wasted on someone who was never going to be a team player. Type A assholes are always a team of one.

CHAPTER 23

PASS THE AGGRESSIVE

Sent: January 13, 10:30 a.m.
From: Alisson
To: Brenda, CEO & Founder
Subject: 1:1?

Hi, Brenda.

Alisson here from Accounting. At the last staff meeting you said that if anyone had any questions they wanted to discuss with you directly, you'd make yourself available. Well, I do have some questions. I was wondering if you'd be willing to have lunch with me sometime.

Alisson

Sent: January 20, 1:30 a.m.
From: Alisson
To: Brenda, CEO & Founder
Subject: 1:1?

Hi, Brenda.

Thank you for lunch! It was so great. You're the best boss ever, even though you're my boss's boss's boss. Ha! It was so interesting learning more about the company strategy. Thanks again!

Alisson

Sent: February 8, 9:00 a.m.
From: Alisson
To: Brenda, CEO & Founder
Subject: 1:1?

Hi, Brenda.

Hi. Me again. Was wondering if you were free for coffee next week? I'd love to share some feedback I have about the new break room decor.

Alisson

Sent: March 5, 8:00 a.m.
From: Alisson
To: Brenda, CEO & Founder
Subject: 1:1?

Hi, Brenda.

I haven't heard back from you. I also wanted to talk to you about my performance review that Tom gave me this morning. I don't think it went very well, which was a surprise. I thought you and I were on the same page. Can you talk to him?

Alisson

Congratulations! You've got an employee stalker! A sure sign of your success is when you've got low-level employees beating down your door in a sad attempt to bond with you. This is almost always—no, it IS always—an attempt to bypass their direct relationship with their manager to get you to play favorites so that when they are finally called out by their own manager, they can come whining to you. But you can work this to your advantage! Play right along with the stalker; they will tell you every last glorious bit of juicy gossip from within the ranks, deliver unto you both good and bad news before you were meant to hear it, and most importantly sell out your most senior leaders by subverting their positions on the ol' org chart and mainlining directly into your already blurry view of your team.

It will start most innocently. You'll meet for lunch. Then she'll ask you for coffee a few times a week. It will be tough to say no because she was quick to achieve a level of familiarity that makes it seem perfectly normal for her to just show up in your doorway unannounced. She'll pounce on you in the break room, the elevator, maybe even the bathroom. She'll prod you for information, drop bread crumbs of her own gossip that will keep you up at night. Before you know it, she will be giving you body-language and eye-contact signals at group meetings and presentations—as if the two of you have "something special."

All the while, because you are too busy getting sucked into her drama, you don't even realize she's on a performance-improvement fast track with her manager. Unless she starts performing her core duties, she's going to be terminated. And all of this has been her strategy for avoiding that inevitable event.

LET'S GET REAL

The next thing you know, you wake up one day to this:

GLASSDOOR ANONYMOUS REVIEW

The ABC Company

CEO Rating: 0 out of 5

The ABC Company, specifically because of their no-talent and lazy CEO, is the worst place to work on the planet. I would rather break rocks in a nuclear test site than set foot in that godforsaken hellhole. The pay is crap, the hours are crap, it's a swampy cesspool of gossip, and the do-nothing CEO is worthless. The company has no strategy, and I'm pretty sure they are out of money also. Every single employee hates it there. It's a revolving door of misery. Not only are their CEO, senior management, and culture in general complete disasters, their product is a sham. It's nothing more than a straight rip-off of the competition's, and they'll ask you to do shady things to try to get even more competitive intel. If you have any dignity or integrity, stay away!

Why the abuse? Because your stalker was finally fired by her manager, and this is exactly how she's going to repay *you directly* for not preventing it.

Listen, unless you want to manage a team of cat herders in the wild, wild West, if you want to develop solid leaders, you have to be the shining example on the hill of order, protocol, and respect for the org chart. Most employees aren't stalkers or subversive people like Alisson, but they are out there. Unless you are consistent about how you interact with your staff, they will find a way to bore into your resolve and then come screaming back in a most public way.

There is a way for you to be friendly—even well liked—without subverting the org chart and allowing these fissures to crack the system. If you feel that an employee or team member is subverting the org chart, direct them back to their manager or hold a group meeting with the three of you. Forming a triad at the first sight of this kind of activity is a great way to fortify your hierarchy.

Remember, one of our most important jobs as a leader is to develop new and better leaders. Every employee—even the Alissons of the world—has the potential to be a leader or influencer, but most don't really understand the value and purpose of a well-crafted, disciplined chain of command. Work with your HR department if you have one, and if not, work regularly with your senior management team to communicate protocol, design, and adhere to RACI methodologies, and stop breaches of org chart protocol in their tracks before you too are victimized or sucked in by one of the many Crazy Alissons!

CHAPTER 24

SOCIAL IRRESPONSIBILITY

You're Invited!

What: A Dinner Party/Fundraiser
Why: To Support Anytown's Homeless Population
Where: The Estate of Our Founder, Bill Brookstone,
in South Highlands

Please join us for an evening of wine, dinner, and song.
Our homeless population is important to us,
so we at Brookstone Realty
want to do our part to support shelters and programs
for the homeless in our city.

Catered by celebrity chef Rich Richardson, dinner will be
a fantastic Asian-fusion exploration of fresh sushi and
seafood. Wines will be paired by our
very own sommelier, Susan Sheppard.

Dinner will be followed by a special private performance
by world-renowned violinist Jen Chen.

Tickets: $250 each

Tables for 6: $1,350 (save $250!)

All additional donations will be
matched 100% by Brookstone Realty!

As leaders, it's important that we stay connected to our communities, contribute to our communities, and make it appear as if we care about the communities in which we live. Holding fundraisers and events is a fantastic way to demonstrate your commitment and leadership without taking too much of a hit to the bottom line. The above is a perfect example of how to put together a fabulous party that you and your guests will enjoy immensely while giving you the opportunity to host a party in your home with top-of-the-line service providers and entertainers. Also, it's 100 percent paid for and can be written off! Win-win!

You can invite community leaders and industry leaders, and while they won't be able to afford to come, you can even extend the invitation to your employees. They'll see not only that you're generous, but that you have great taste in food and music. By selling tickets, you're simply covering your costs. You can ask for donations, but because most guests will think that the cost of their ticket is donated, they won't make extra donations, and your claim of matching donations 100 percent will sound so, so much better than it really is. You may actually get to pull this scheme off and turn a little profit!

LET'S GET REAL

Oh yeah, there's nothing like holding a fundraiser for the homeless in the estate of a real estate tycoon.

Seriously, this seems absurd, but when it comes to "social responsibility" leaders really can be this tone deaf. *Social responsibility* is a term popularized over the last several years that has become a mainstay of good corporate stewardship. It is supposed to be defined by what your company believes is its responsibility to society and what it does to support that belief. Key word here: *believes*.

It is one thing to simply throw some money at some charities, then spin up some marketing-speak to make it sound like your company is run by do-gooders. It's another thing to actually believe in something, communicate that belief genuinely to both your staff and the community, then execute strategies and tactics to stay true to those beliefs. Example:

Belief: At Brookstone Realty, we believe that everyone needs to feel at home.

Strategy: We'll donate 5 percent of our annual profits to programs that help build shelters and homes for those in need.

Tactics: Twice a year, for one day, we close our offices as our staff joins Habitat for Humanity to participate in building homes.

See how easy it is? Much easier than throwing a fancy party that nobody on your staff can participate in. Habitat for Humanity wins, your company wins by being true to a belief, and your staff wins by feeling like they achieved a common goal. THAT, dear leaders, is a win-win-win.

Each year, as part of your strategic planning process, design a social responsibility platform for the year. First, decide on a maximum percentage of net income that you or your owners are comfortable with earmarking for charitable donations. Once that amount is agreed on, do not change it until the following year. Then create a pie chart showing the allocation of percentages. You can have each department take on a piece of the pie, or you could decide that some of it will be straight cash donations and some of it will be employee time off to volunteer with special charities. However you construct your platform, make sure it is inclusive and genuine. At the end of the year you and the staff can include it in your list of accomplishments, or "goals met," for the year.

Nothing bonds a group of people together like meeting shared goals. And a goal of giving that is shared and believed in by all can be part of a very powerful brand story.

- Do I have a social responsibility platform that has been clearly communicated to the company?

- Does the platform have some conceptual relationship to the mission of the company?

- Are there enough opportunities within that platform to give my staff options to get involved?

- Can the staff get involved without spending any money, and is their time just as valuable to the cause?

- Does anything about the platform feel mandatory or expected?

ABOUT THE AUTHORS

Mary Marshall's passion is helping entrepreneurs and executives achieve their dreams. Mary has been a CEO, an owner, and chief cook and bottle washer. She's been a Vistage Chair (member and executive) and has coached leaders to find their own success. In 2014, she published her first book, *Putting Together the Entrepreneurial Puzzle: The Ten Pieces Every Business Needs to Succeed* as a collection of answers to the most common problems that hamper small business success. Marshall Advisors, LLC is Mary's consulting practice in Seattle, which focuses on strategic planning, CEO and executive coaching, and leadership development. Mary speaks on Intentional Culture for organizations nationally. Since 2012, she has been active teaching a course for the Small Business Administration called "Emerging Leaders" that takes entrepreneurs through a seven-month course to create a strategic growth plan for their businesses. The course is considered a mini MBA.

Kim Obbink is an Art Center College of Design graduate who began her career as a graphic designer and over the years became an accomplished brand strategist and leader. She worked as both employee and vendor for many worldclass technology and entertainment companies, and ultimately served as CEO of a Seattle based digital marketing and talent acquisition company. Her experience brings high-altitude vision and strong brand strategy to everything she does. Kim believes that an authentic brand requires authentic leadership. Her vision that values and a well-stated, well-actioned belief system are the religion of every healthy organization is what she brings to her consulting work with growth-oriented companies today. An entrepreneur, strategist, writer, and artist, Kim has a colorful view of the world. That combined with a bold sense of humor allow her to share her unique perspective on how others can find success and satisfaction in being great leaders from the heart.

CPSIA information can be obtained
at www.ICGtesting.com
Printed in the USA
BVHW041759210920
589297BV00012B/171